REFLECTIONS ON SHAKESPEARE AND NEWTON

REFLECTIONS ON SHAKESPEARE AND NEWTON

Their Cultural Legacy for Today

Robert L. Wormell

VANTAGE PRESS
New York ● Los Angeles

Published by Vantage Press, Inc.
516 West 34th Street, New York, New York 10001

Manufactured in the United States of America
ISBN: 0-533-08856-9

Library of Congress Catalog Card No.: 89-90525

1 2 3 4 5 6 7 8 9 0

To my grandchildren,
Catherine, Jill, and Christopher Max

Contents

Preface

We should all like to make sense of our lives, and to feel that we were cooperating in a drive towards a more unified, yet at the same time, more individually liberated society. There are two main avenues towards this goal. One way is to delve into the past in order to discover those guides which our ancestors considered important. Even these should be suitably modified to bring them into line with restless change. The other way is to examine the physical world in an effort to bring all its observable evidence into one simplified and unified world-picture.

Unfortunately the two front-runners of physics : Relativity and Planck's Quantum Theory of Action, are both in a bad way. Relativity is in disarray because its two parallel theories, Special and General, contradict each other. No effort has yet been made to reconcile them. The Special Theory demonstrated the algebraic consequences, $E = mC^2$, of the Fitzgerald contraction. This was the very important finding that the Earth contracts and expands about six inches every day owing to its revolution round the Sun. It orbits at 18.5 miles per second. Special Relativity visualises everything following parallel 'world-lines,' like those of longitude, running on to infinity in determinist fashion. The later General Theory supposed that the universe was finite but unbounded, in an effort to explain universal expansion.

Planck's theory of 'action' is the other theory in distress. We have to be careful about action because here it does not mean, as in general usage, the simple ebullition of energy, or the rate of doing work. It is quite the opposite. In a technical sense, it is termed the product, not the dividend of energy with time. Energy is work, the result of force acting through a distance. As we all know force

ix

is mass times acceleration. So, in the shorthand of algebra, action becomes m.a.l.t., where m stands for *mass*, a for *acceleration*, l for *length*, and t for *time*. Acceleration itself is the rate of change of velocity : l/t^2.

So action boils down to: ml^2t^{-1}. These symbols, ml^2t^{-1}, according to the text-books, are the dimensions of 'action. Similarly energy becomes ml^2t^{-2}. It all seems very neat and tidy. But while energy, ml^2t^{-2}, and all the other quantities of mechanics can be translated back into rational pictures, ml^2t^{-1}, the dimensions of action get—nowhere. You cannot visualise a point-mass moving along two transverse lengths at one and the same time. The whole concept is a nonsense. Any theory of action is not in accord with either nature or science. Yet we all instinctively feel that because mass and energy are equivalent, that energy ought to be particulate and to divide into units, atoms of energy. We have demonstrated how this can be in Chapter 6, "The Nature of Cooling."

With the plight of Relativity and Quantum Theories, we seem to have reached a final impasse. Yet all the time, more and more empirical evidence has been steadily accumulating. We might take a short step backwards to advance even further forwards. The time is ripe for a single unifying idea like those of Shakespeare and Newton. One which might tie everything together into a satisfactory whole. The book tries to do this.

I should like to thank my son, Christopher, and my daughter, Angela, for much assistance in the writing.

Winfield,
British Columbia
27 September 1989

REFLECTIONS ON
SHAKESPEARE
AND NEWTON

Introduction

*They are slaves who dare not be
in the right with two or three.*
—J. Russell Lowell

Writing about oneself is distasteful; but some sort of description
seems desirable. My mother was fairly old, thirty-six, and my father
was thirty-seven, when I was born on 29 October 1901. It was a
day when the Caesarewich was won in a snowstorm; my mother
also said it was snowing that morning. The only other time I can
remember it snowing on my birthday was in 1943. I remarked to
a colleague, Dr. Harry Paul, who was lunching with me, that it was
snowing on my forty-second birthday; and he replied that it was
also his birthday. Curiously I have never found anyone else with
the same birthday; although I must have spoken to many at some
time or other.

I got my first names in a peculiar way. My father's name was
Robert, but this was common in the family. Although my parents
inclined to Robert, they were looking for another name to go with
it. At the time, my parents had been reading, and were enthralled
with *Treasure Island* by Robert Louis Stevenson; thus they thought
"Robert Louis" was the answer. I never liked either my first or
family names. "Louis" seemed French and feminine. And when I
went to school, other boys would shout; "Wormhole, Wormhole
fell down a worm-hole." Later, I discovered a number of people
of a similar name: Wormall, living in Lancashire and Yorkshire.
The name appears to be a neologism from that of a Norman follower of the conquerer; Roger de Wormele, who was mentioned
in the *Doomsday Book*.

A superficial appraisal of the lives of Shakespeare and Newton
may give the impression that they both completed fairly calm,
happy, and successful lives. Shakespeare was well esteemed at Strat-

1

ford-upon-Avon, Warwickshire, where he retired toward the end of his life. Newton also seemed to have everything going for him. Even as a young man, he was elected a Fellow of Trinity College in Cambridge; then admitted to the Royal Society, which went on to elect him its president. Later, he became master of the mint, and was knighted by Queen Anne in 1705. In fact both lives were probably clouded and distorted by clerical opposition. Yet both form landmarks in a true Christian succession. Both show facets akin to those in the New Testament to which they form an enlightened sequel.

Newton shows a likeness to Shakespeare in that they both appear to have published under duress. They both had important contributions to make to humanism, and they both came up against the sinister forces of repression. This is why their efforts are still hazy with uncertainty. There is no doubt that a person known as Shakespeare lived at Stratford-upon-Avon in Warwickshire, U.K.; and that he made frequent journeys to and from London; probably up the Stour, down the Evenlode, to Bruen Abbey; then on to the Thames via Oxford. But there is doubt concerning the origin of the group of famous plays attributed to him, which appeared between a short interval, 1590–1600. Shakespeare's central unifying idea was "The Globe"; and his works are full of the old three-tier picture of life as on a stage.

Newton's contribution concerned motion and force, as emphasised in the laws of motion (*Principia*). But the theological implication of acceleration are still repressed. Acceleration implies will; and will starts in the mind and brain. Yet the whole physical universe is in constant acceleration; because its ultimate particles are waves, and waves are defined as accelerations about a mean. Thus the universe and all existence is built from a confluence of jostling thought and its resultant concentration into deeds; and this is Newton's central theme.

In 1927, the bi-centenary of his death, Newton's private letters were published according to his instructions. They were opened and sold to J. M. Keynes, who was then regarded as the apotheosis of finance. Like Einstein, his theories are now the worse for wear. But Keynes, who might have praised Newton, was content to berate.

Newton was said to have wasted half his life with vain attempts at alchemy. Keynes must have known that Newton was master of the mint in the days before the advent of chemistry. Pewter, an alloy of tin, lead, copper, and antimony, at that time was considered to resemble silver. It seemed a fair ambition to transmute base metals. In any case, fundamental science is indivisible. Chemistry and physics are really one subject. Nitrogen triboride closely resembles the diamond, with a similar, tetrahedral, electronic structure. Research is like fishing—you have to be prepared to toil all night and catch nothing. Yet negative results can be as important as positive. To sum up, we should pay more regard to Cowper's verdict—to give Newton some of the great respect he once had during the eighteenth century.

When I first started to try to improve the properties of rayon, by stretching, I was intrigued by a very old principle—Hooke's Law, which says that "stretch is always directly proportional to strain." Why should tension sharply increase on stretching? A fiber, just like any other matter, is made up of opposite electric charges, which always attract each other flexibly. So superficially, you might expect all solid objects to be naturally elastic; as though they were made of rubber. How might the rigidity of solids arise? We have to think that rigidity is largely the result of rigid positive nuclei. The rings produced by a succession of positively charged carbon atoms, do not lie in one plane; a benzene ring is crenellated. Just as we had to think that a lump of sugar placed in water dissolved and led to a "sugar-gas;" so we have to think that the dispersion of electrons inside a metal object forms an electron gas. The only difference from air is that electrons disperse into both space and time. Similarly the electrons in any solid, not only in metals, may move not only in space, but in time as well; making four dimensions in all. Hence Stefan's Law: The energy radiated by a hot body is proportional to the fourth power of the temperature, $E = Kt^4$, where t is the absolute temperature, E is the energy radiated, and K is Stefan's constant.

The freely moving electron gas also clarifies Hooke's Law of stress and strain; which is really a special case of Newton's more generalised third law: To every action there is an equal and opposite reaction. Hooke was a contemporary of Newton; in fact he preceded the latter as president of the Royal Society. Hooke claimed to have anticipated Newton's views as the originator of universal gravitation. The only thing missing from Hooke's ideas was their lack of exact mathematical correlation. Newton's superior mathematics clarified gravity beyond doubt. His third law is not merely confined to science; it underlies everything that happens in the whole of existence!

Thus Newtonian dynamics led on to the kinetic theory of gases. You can actually find out how fast the particles of a gas, such as air, are moving, simply by finding their pressure. The easiest way is to imagine them separated into six equal and similar streams, up and down, down and up, left to right, right to left, back to front, and front to back. The combined change of momentum of any stream makes up the atmospheric pressure, known to be 760 dynes per sq centimeter. Rough arithmetic shows that molecules of air are moving at 1,000 mph and hydrogen molecules at about 4,000 mph. Stefan's Law suggests that electrons are always in thermodynamic equilibrium with their surroundings. Because a proton has 1,838 times more inertia than an electron, we might expect the mean speed of the latter to be ca. 1838 times the former. Thus an electron could oscillate 136 times faster than an associated proton, yet take only a quarter share of all increments of energy. Despite all the advances made in spectroscopy and the fine structure of spectral lines, as well as proliferated theories of atomic structure, there is still a common persistence in picturing electrons as though they were in orbit; a visualisation that is as out of date as the "Saturnian" atom of the nineteenth century. The only idea that makes sense around the nucleus is extension in four dimensions. We shall see later that "dead-beat" time might supply that fourth dimension and place everything in a new light. If Newton were alive today, he would want to know what progress had been made in his concept of the ruthless passage of time. The vision of time as a tidal wave may seem far removed from Shakespearean drama, but in his last play, *The Tempest*, he speaks of "the cloud-capped

4

towers, the gorgeous palaces, the solemn temples and the great globe itself," dissolving to "leave not a wrack behind."

When the Dissolution of the Monastries was announced in 1532, it must have brought a great trauma to Coventry. What exactly happened to the dispersed monks, and particularly to their almsgiving social services, is not recorded (see Chapter 3).

Longfellow's *Theologian's Tale* sets the scene. A monk is undecided, whether to stay and watch a developing vision; or to obey the summons of the abbey bell, proclaiming the time for the distribution of alms. When he returns from the distribution, an hour later, the vision is still there.

> "Hadst thou stayed, I must have fled,"
> That is what the Vision said.

It is probable that many monks were helped by the established churches. But every national upheaval is likely to start off trains of thought. The displaced monks must have considered what they ought to do with the accumulated archives and history of their own abbey and that of the surrounding district. Coventry is known to have been a centre for the performance of the "Morality Plays," elementary stories of dramatised moral principles, which had emerged over the years. It is not hard to imagine, given the repression then the vogue, the sad fate of anything resembling mere amusement, performed on a raised platform, such as a stage. Any such activities had to remain closely secret. It was probably soon realised that some of the outstanding material was too precious to be lost. The period immediately following the reign of Henry VIII was exceedingly dangerous for innovators; and not until the death of "Bloody Mary" was there any hope of publication.

I first heard the suggestion, at the tercentenary of his death in 1916, that Shakespeare's works originated in monasteries. By the gradual accumulation of hints from many sources and incidents, the idea has been confirmed. I remember, about the year 1960, walking through a wild area of Coombe park soon after it had been taken over by Coventry Corporation for the provision of a nature trail. The ancestral owners, since the dissolution, had been the earls of Craven. About the year 1900 the then earl had married an American heiress. He had become enthusiastic about the idea of bringing over to his estate a selection of trees native to America: maples and redwoods (sequoa). As I walked through the trail in 1970, I noticed a tall tree that stood about eighty feet high, similar to those portrayed in children's books. It showed a wide trunk, with tapering peak. I believe it was a redwood in its early years. The preservation of trees is a noble idea. But the two families, the Cravens and the Leighs, who were rewarded by Henry VIII with large grants of land near Coventry, have not particularly distinguished themselves in history books. In fact I believe they have each suffered a series of misfortunes through the years; it reminds us of the legendary curse suposed to have been made by the dispossessed monks.

About 1850, the then Lord Leigh donated sandstone from Stoneleigh Deer Park for the erection of two twin churches in Coventry: Saint Thomas's and All Saints. These were later demolished because of their erosion, probably caused by acid rain. Their sandstone was too soft; but they had lasted over a hundred years. Lord Leigh also initiated a textile factory, the Leigh Mills, to help the unemployed silkweavers of Huguenot extraction. A number of Coventry charities and schools were endowed by medieval benefactors. In fact, around 1910 a noted trades-unionist came to Coventry and said that the town was "born, bred and fed on charity." My father went to the Green Gift School, and my uncle to the Blue Gift. Later, four gift schools were amalgamated with the old Bablake School, and then, later still, with the King Henry VIII School, to form the present Coventry School. In addition medieval Coventry comprised several guilds, the prototypes of trades-unions: Trinity Guild, the guild of capers and feltmakers. The city was, in the Middle Ages, an important textile centre, where sheep-farming had become a large industry. The British lord chancellor, by tradition, sits on the wool-sack because wool was once an important source of revenue. It was then a sore point around Coventry that so much wool was exported as tribute to the See of Rome. Witness the protestations of John Wycliffe (1320—1384) of Lutterworth near Coventry. The city has been a Protestant, Anglican and republican centre throughout history.*

A mile west of the city centre lies the Templars Fields, still an open space. Further to the west (six miles) is the village of Temple Balsall. The Knights Templar once claimed this as their centre. Clockwise to the north (five miles) is Maxstoke Priory. To the east (four miles) are the Coombe fields and abbey; Lutterworth is only eight miles farther east. Southeast half a mile from the city centre stands The Charter House, once a monastery established by Richard II. A mile farther southeast along the London Road is Whitley Abbey, standing at the confluence of the rivers Sowe and Sherbourne. To the south and southwest are Stoneleigh and Kenilworth Abbeys. Much evidence of the monastic period remains in the form of local street names; Palmer Lane, Priory Row, Greyfriars Green, Whitefriars Cloisters, and many others.

Lord Tennyson describes in his famous poem "Godiva" how "he watched the three tall spires." In medival days there were six, not three spires, clustered together. Three arose from Saint Mary's cathedral, which was structured like Lichfield Cathedral, only Saint Mary's was the larger. All this evidence points to a restlessness and repression, a fermentation of ideas taking place in an isolated yet celibate community, an incipient medieval monastic university. In fact, some funds arising from the Dissolution were deducted by Henry VIII to found colleges at Oxford and Cambridge.

The introduction of printing by Caxton in 1476 accelerated the crystallisation of the English language. Its complete formation took place over the relatively short period between 1400 and 1550. The Dissolution (1532) thus came at the formative climax. It is noteworthy that scraps of Elizabethan literature discovered from time to time are often claimed as Shakespearean. Whereas, because

---

*Prof. G. M. Trevelyan, of Oxford University says, "Martin Luther, leader of the Reformation of Western Christendom, was greatly influenced by Jan Hus of Prague, Bohemia. Hus, in turn was an earlier pupil of John Wycliffe (1320—1384) of Lutterworth. This town is eight miles east of Coombe Fields, the focus of the Craven Estates. Thus we may feel that Saint Mary's, Coventry was a source of the Reformation." It is quite significant that there is the village of Monks Kirby, four miles east of Coombe and four miles west of Lutterworth.

7

The Burning of Laurence Sanders, 1555

the language was just out of the melting pot, all writing was that much more conventional, and thus showed an affinity with Shakespeare. This is why we believe that more than one author had a hand in the works.

During the short reign of "Bloody Mary," Protestants were being sent to the stake all over the place. There is an old monument at Parkside, near the city centre, devoted to the memory of the Coventry Martyrs. Fourteen were burned in Coventry, two sent for burning in Manchester, and one died in prison (see illustrations). Thus it was that not until Elizabeth I appeared (1558), that a new era began. The people loved the new queen because she retained all the elan of her father, Henry VIII, coupled with her natural femininity and discretion. So suddenly there appeared the hope for a better and more rewarding life. The sixteenth century saw the discovery of the New World. Britain, being a predominantly maritime nation, was only too ready to accept the challenge of an expanded vision. Shakespeare's dates (1564—1616) fall at the peak of this cultural upsurge. Shakespeare began with historical plays about fighting and war. It is therefore surprising that he makes no mention of the rout of the Spanish Armada (1588). During James I's (1603—1616) reign he was mostly sterile.

We might suppose that behind closed doors, and over many years, traditional dramatic enactments of histories, episodes, and fables were realised unknown to the outside world. Later a strong, young local agent had to be found; fit enough to ride out; picking up material from half a dozen local monasteries; yet determined and mature enough to make long and arduous journeys to London. Shakespeare of Stratford upon Avon was just the man; approaching thirty years old, a well-trained actor, yet familiar with the deceptive, naughty outside world. This we believe was the truth concerning the mystery of Shakespeare (see Chapter 2).

Chapter 1

The Eclipse of Newton

Patient in correction, as a child,
Affable, humble, diffident and mild.
Such was Sir Isaac.
                    —William Cowper

The appraisal of the works of eminent authors nearly always follows a sort of sine curve: their reputations go up and down like a switchback. Thus their prestige usually declines during a lapse of about fifty to one hundred years after their deaths. For example, the reputations of a number of great Victorian writers are said to have been "debunked,' but more recently some are beginning to find a rising trend. Newton was very successful and famous around the beginning of the eighteenth century, right up to his death in 1727. But later, especially on the continent, his scientific dominance began to decline. Thus there appeared a rise in the static tradition of mechanics during the latter half of the eighteenth century. Then D'Alembert (1717–1783) and Lagrange (1736–1813) introduced the principle of "least action," while Gauss (1777–1855) brought "least constraint." Newtonian mechanics was later severely criticised by Ernst Mach (1832–1916) and J. H. Poincare (1854–1912).

What is the fundamental source of the dynamics/statics clash? The answer is given by J. M. E. McTaggart (1908). He described two alternative ways of thinking about time: According to the A series, time may be thought of as that flux and transiency that gives rise to the tenses, the process of temporal becoming, the gnawing tooth of time. Or, as stated in the B series, time may be regarded as a "pattern of timeless moments." Events are laid out in a static, tenseless way, a democratic equality for all times. The A theory is favoured by philosophers C. D. Broad, L. S. Stebbing, J. Wisdom, P. F. Marhenke, A. H. Prior, W. Sellars, S. Hampshire, P. F. Strawson, and J. N. Findlay. The defenders of the B theory are mostly logical atomists or positivists, or rational reconstructionists. Their preeminent advocate is Bertrand Russell, followed by R. B. Braithwaite, C. D. Ducasse, A. Grunbaum, A. J. Ayer, W. V. Quine, N. Goodman, D. C. Williams, J. C. Smart, and R. D. Bradley. These authors are professors of scientific philosophy. So the intellectual division between A and B theories is about equal. Mathematicians and physicists seem to support the B series because of recent scientific history.

Time is so fundamental to science that we ought to look for any logical argument in support of the A theory. We realise that dynamics (A series) has also a long history culminating with Newton. His science was based on salient principles. Thus his definition of time clearly takes him into the A camp: "Absolute, true, and mathematical time, of itself and from its own nature, flows equably without relation to anything external." This flow of time was attacked by Einstein, who argued that time merged with space to form a space/time continuum. You would be equally right to say that the sun was eight minutes away, as to say that it was 96 million miles away. What he missed was the basic finding that there are three dimensions to the physical world: mass, space, and time, and that mass acts transversely to space and time. It follows that becoming must move at the speed of light.

The B series protagonists do not explain the intrinsic might of the present tense, particularly its synchronisation with natural intervals: the sequence of days and nights, the seasons, the swings of a pendulum, or the stresses and recoveries of a hairspring. For them everything follows on, is geometrically predestined and laid down, and sealed and inevitable as a clockwork. On the other hand Newtonian dynamics has, in fact, doubled its scope. This advance has been, intentionally or unintentionally, overlooked by the B series apologists. It is never explained in elementary books of physics that Newton's three laws and his three fundamental equations of motion apply not just to idealistic, uniform, straight-line transference, but also to the more important general angular rotation. The defiance of gravity by the spinning gyroscope is never properly cleared up. It is not conceded that a body gains in mass by revolution. In fact, straight-line motion is hypothetical: most astronomical bodies move in approximate circles.

Two past events stand out starkly in my recollections of Newton. The first was when I visited Birmingham University, Edgbaston, in 1918 to take the practical test for inter B. Sc. (Physics). The set question was to carry out observations of the rate of fall in the temperature of water in a beaker, to plot the temperatures against times, and thus to verify Newton's law of cooling, which states that "The rate of cooling is proportional to the excess temperature above the surroundings." This simple correlation is based on an exponential curve, which at zero temperature approximates to a hyperbola. I was puzzled about the matter because I took it that Newton's cooling law had been discovered by trial and error; nobody had pointed out a rationale. Over the years I gradually began to realise how, in fact, it logically follows on from Newtonian dynamics. Newton has had a very bad press over this. You won't find anything about it in modern dictionaries or encyclopedias. Most biographies confine their attention to his mathematical prowess, to his laws of motion, and to his prismatic analysis of white light. There seems to have been an unfortunate tendency to forget Newton's law of cooling. Even about diffraction he has been badly misrepresented. It is true that his original single, corpuscular theory, which naturally followed closely his views about the nature of atoms and their conservation, was modified when he heard the reactions of Huygens, Hooke, and others. Thus he assigned different masses for corpuscules corresponding to different wavelengths. He followed up with the idea of diffraction as the rationale for Newton's rings. These, of course, are circular, coloured patterns produced when a spot of oil on a plane surface is deformed by the pressure of curved glass.

During the whole of the nineteenth century Newton was criticised for his corpuscular theory, when Young's wave theory became the vogue; this followed on along with the luminiferous ether. Later came the modern quantum theory, which saw light both as particles and waves (photons) according to probabilities. Photons approximate closely to Newton's original corpuscles. It provides another instance of that dip in prestige so often encountered by eminent authors shortly after death. What ought to be said, is that it is now time to give Newton a bit more respect. For example, it should be pointed out that the quantum theory itself was partially anticipated by Newton's law of cooling. The basic quantum equation is:

$$E \times \lambda = h;$$

where E is the radiant energy generated, the wavelength λ, and h Planck's quantum or constant of action : 6.554×10^{-27} ergs per second. This relation gives a succession of minute zones, which together form the outlines of a simple hyperbola. Of course quantum theory confines itself to radiant energy, whereas Newton's cooling embraces all forms of heat: radiant, conductive, and convection. And the reasoning behind Newton's law is equally simple. All matter exists as ultimate particles, and these move either en masse: convection by continuously colliding; conduction; or by electric oscillation or radiation. In a word, heat is just molecular motion. Newton had earlier proved that the energy of a moving particle is proportional to both its mass and the square of its velocity. In this way, temperature resolves itself into the mean velocity of constituent molecules. Thus, in effect, Newton is the founder, not only of dynamics, but also of thermodynamics, and later electrodynamics, or roughly the whole of modern physics.

Why has Newton's work been so clouded and dimmed? This brings me to the second vivid moment. In 1919 I was on the 8:22 A.M. train to New Street, Birmingham, when I saw in the *Times* the results of Professor Arthur Eddington's expedition to Samoa to observe a total eclipse of the sun. A new theory on the nature of time and existence had been substantiated by the extraordinary observation that light from a fixed star, grazing a limb of the sun during the eclipse, had actually been deflected by the sun's intense gravitation. This was an electric finding that had been quantitatively predicted by a German professor by the name of Albert Einstein.

13

It seemed to have undermined not only the efforts of Newton, but the whole of exact knowledge.

Of course very few experts were then able to explain what the new theory was all about. I was an undergraduate at the time, and I saw a notice that Mr. Sydney Webb, later Lord Passfield, was to give a lecture on Socialism and Relativity. The gist of the talk was simply that "Everything depends on the accepted framework of reference." Webb instanced the rule of the road. He contended that some regulation of traffic had to be formulated to prevent chaos: a small concession to tyranny produced a great gain of freedom. Einstein actually claimed that "Any one given framework was as good as any other," which, of course, promotes democracy to absurdity. Tom's frame was as good as Dick's frame, which, in turn, was as good as Harry's.

Einstein went on to visualize a universe infinite in space and time, his basic space/time continuum: parallel lines extending into both infinite past and infinite future; thus visualising an absolutely static and dead cosmos. Later he evolved a picture of space/time curving back on itself, finite but unbounded. Sir Arthur Eddington, a follower of Einstein, claimed that this curving universe required twelve imaginary dimensions, together with sixteen radii of curvature.* In 1920 Einstein published *Relativity*, a popular explanation of his theories. The book was described by the author as "intended for those who are not conversant with the math of theoretical physics." He seems to have had an obsessive antipathy to Newton. He even goes as far as calling the principles of dynamics, Galilei-Newton.

There are thirty-six references to Galileo or a Galilean system in the book, with only fourteen to Newton. Newton was born the year Galileo died. The latter certainly made many important astronomical discoveries. He called attention to the importance of inertia, and dropped feathery and dense bodies from the leaning tower of Pisa, constructed a practicable telescope, observed spots on the Sun, craters on the Moon, resolved the stars of the Milky Way, found the rings of Saturn and its spheroidal shape, and saw

*Arthur Stanley Eddington, *The Nature of the Physical World* (London).

the four large satellites of Jupiter. Galileo passionately believed that the Sun was at the centre of the solar system. Yet it was Newton who collected most of the data together and united it with his three basic equations. In this way he set up a vastly simplified picture of existence. During his lifetime he was often engaged in scientific controversy: with Descartes, who had evolved a rival view of the universe and gravity; with Hooke, who also claimed to have originated the idea of universal attraction; with Liebnitz, who claimed to have initiated the calculus; and with Huygens, who first believed that light was a form of wave motion. But never in his generation did anyone approaching Newton's calibre see Galileo as the founder of dynamics.

Newton was an innovator, who not only introduced a more economical way of looking at the physical world, but more importantly, was one whose ideas could be accepted by ordinary people. In sharp contrast, general relativity saw the universe as the infinite surface of a flat ocean—the space/time continuum. This picture did not bear inspection, so it had to be contorted through many imaginary dimensions into a one-piece superficial shell, which in a way, was difficult to understand. In its early days of the 1920s, some astronomers claimed to have sighted a dim and distant object, which was said to be an image of our own galaxy reflected from the shell-like other side of the universe. Little has been heard of this idea in recent years. On the other hand, the cosmos has been found to be more extensive than even relativity could predict, but the general theory saw it expanding like a soap bubble.

Newton's view of the cosmos was, in effect, diametrically opposed to that of relativity, because he had himself speculated that its density should increase owing to the attractive effect of gravity. Experimentation is the real and deciding test of theory. In this respect the development of both optical and radio telescopes has resolved the conflict in favour of Newton. As telescopes have improved, it became possible to glimpse far into the deepest past. This has now been found to have been proportionally more populated with galaxies. We saw earlier that Einstein's final theory described the universe as an expanding film, rather like a bulging soap bubble, but in 1920 Abbé Lemaitre had proposed that it began with a great explosion: the big bang theory. Matter was rapidly dispersed far and wide to all points of the sky, starting from a primeval atom, the focal origin. The only contention with this theory was that of Fred Hoyle, who proposed the idea of "continuous creation" throughout the wide spaces between the stars. In fact, in recent years optical and radio observation has clearly demonstrated that all galaxies are receding from a single point at speeds directly proportional to their remoteness in the depths of space (Hubble's law).

The most common element to appear with the big bang theory was positively charged hydrogen gas (protons along with their attendant electrons). Thus the immediate effect was an intense emission of E/M light from the depths of space, arriving from all points of the sky. This radiation, deep in the infra-red, and indicating recession near velocity, C, exemplified both the Balmer and Lyman series.

Einstein devotes Chapter XXX, the first chapter in Part III of his book, to "Cosmological Difficulties of Newton's Theory." The writer summarizes: "However far we might travel through space, we should find everywhere an attenuated swarm of fixed stars of approximately the same kind and density." He then says, "This view is not in harmony with the theory of Newton, which requires the universe to have a centre." By about 1950, the soap-bubble universe of Einstein had become untenable, leaving only two contenders: 1) the continuous creation theory of Fred Hoyle, and 2) the big bang theory originated by Lemaitre.

Today the lapse of time and a mass of astronomical observations has confirmed the big bang theory. But conventional physicists are still reluctant to face the consequences of increased density towards the centre. In the *Frontiers of Astronomy* by Fred Hoyle, Heineman, 1955, plate XLII: "The Limit to which Man can reach out into Space," shows a swarm of galaxies, a billion parsecs distant. Thirteen faint images are pinpointed, covering only a minute fraction of the heavens. Even more recent observations using radiotelescopes have found E/M radiations up to six times more distant. What could provide a more convincing confirmation of the classic Newtonian view!

Chapter 2

Coventry: Shakespeare's Alma Mater

I waited for the train at Coventry;
I hung with grooms and porters on the bridge,
To watch the three tall spires.

—Tennyson

Most people feel that Stratford-upon-Avon is well documented as Shakespeare's hometown, and they dismiss as unlikely and far-fetched the notion that some other prominent Elizabethan, such as Lord Bacon or Christopher Marlowe, was the real writer. Yet they cannot entirely eliminate from their minds a sinister feeling of mystery, inconsistency, and suppression about the authorship. The tercentenary of Shakespeare's death occurred in 1916, in the middle of the First World War. The distraction of the war prevented any elaborate celebration, but it did engender a lively discussion about the rival claims of Bacon and Marlowe. A curate at Saint Peter's Coventry, the Reverend Jack Puterill, later Vicar of Thaxted in Essex, came out with a suggestion that has received little attention or comment. He said: "Of course the monks wrote it," but gave no supporting facts.

Over the years it has seemed to the writer that this suggestion has become more and more plausible. And it has also seemed more and more likely that Coventry was once the centre for its cerebration. What can be said in favour of this suggestion? To a superficial observer old monasteries may seem to be distributed quite randomly in the Midlands. But more careful consideration shows that there were factors that did have a definite influence on the selection of their position. It may seem mysterious that during the Middle

Ages there was a decided lack of proper roads. Why was this so, seeing that previously during the Roman Occupation, a rudimentary network of important and straight roads was established? The answers throws a sharp light on the evolution of civilisation. The Roman Empire was initially extremely dictatorial and autocratic. When it came to making roads the Romans used slave labour. We get an insight into this in the New Testament when Christ said; "If anyone should compel thee to go with him a mile; go with him twain." It was the custom for Roman soldiers to force local inhabitants to carry baggage. And this servitude, no doubt, greatly helped in the transportation of Roman armies. When Rome was converted to Christianity, a great deal of steam went out of Roman autocracy. Many people think that the fall of the Roman Empire was due to decadent habits; but perhaps it may have been brought about by its exact opposite—mass conversion to Christianity.

It is interesting to compare Christian, Roman Britain with Christian Ireland. The Britons were a conquered race; they became dependent on their masters, the Romans. Ireland was never conquered by Rome; but it was converted to Christianity by missionaries. It thus became a great Christian centre; and it was able to reconvert England long after the latter had become overrun by barbarians. Thus it was that originally, Wales and Ireland took charge of the reconverted Britons and invading Angles; and why the Anglican tradition goes as far back as Rome itself. The kings of England once had the power to reward with grants of land and property those who had proved themselves faithful in times of crisis, war, or rebellion. And so it was that the old nobility of Britain was established. They formed the nucleus of a body of wealthy people responsible for running the feudal system under the rules of Christendom then prevailing. It was natural, in the context of the time, that many powerful and wealthy individuals bequeathed grants of lands and estates to various Church authorities when they died so that eventually about half the kingdom fell under the dominance of the church. In this way there grew up a feeling not unlike that in the American colonies, when the colonists sensed that their resources were being drained by George III. This feeling was originally expressed by Wycliffe, who was in charge of a church at

Lutterworth, not far from Coventry. Later, of course, the feeling burst forth with the coming of the Reformation and the setting up by Henry VIII of the National Church. Rome became the tyrant, the great spider, and was at the centre of a conspiracy to drain the resources of Britain, more particularly its wool, to the continent of Europe.

Why then did medieval Britain not markedly increase its skeleton of roads? The answer lies in the high labour cost of making roads without modern methods. The Romans could afford to be dictatorial; but the more pious converted barbarians could not. Democracy is deep rooted: "Were not all men equal in the sight of God?" In this way the river systems of Britain remained the natural and preferred means of transportation. Which then became the best route out of London to the North? It began with the Thames as far as Oxford; some may even have gone on as far as Burford. But then came the obstacle of the Cotswolds. This did require going overland. But probably the most popular route was a compromise, which avoided the escarpment at Edgehill, and used the crudely canalised Stour at Shipston to take it to Stratford. It is worth noting that there are two Shipstons in these parts: Shipston On Stour and Shipston Under Wychwood. The latter is at the side of the Evenlode, a tributary of the Thames and also near Bruern Abbey only three miles further upriver.

At this time the Avon was also a well-used waterway. Upstream led to the two important castles: Warwick and Kenilworth. Warwick because it commanded further progress upstream, and Kenilworth* because it lay at the point of departure overland to Leicester via Coventry, and further to the whole of the northeast: Derby, Nottingham, and York. At the time Lord Warwick was known as the "kingmaker." Downstream led to the Severn, giving it a link with Wales and the southwest; while the higher reaches led to Shrewsbury and the northwest.

What have river systems to do with monasteries? They were part of the communications between church groups. Thus it is not surprising that they were often established at the confluences of

---

*Sir Walter Scott, in his novel, describes how the men of Coventry presented a masque in honour of Queen Elizabeth, during her visit to the Castle, 1575.

rivers: Tewkesbury, Stoneleigh, Whitley. Even the cloistered origins of Oxford (on the Thames) and Cambridge may owe something of their siting to the confluences with the rivers Cherwell and Granta, respectively. Fellowship was another factor that came into play. The church formed bonds of coherence. Thus the imposing Cathedral of Saint Mary at Coventry was not only a great abbey, but became an intense focus for monastic activity. Built on the lines of Lichfield, but larger; it also formed the centre for a number of satellite abbeys: Coombe, Stoneleigh, Kenilworth, and Maxstoke.

Roads in those days were largely dirt tracks, which rapidly became rutty and waterlogged in winter. The construction of wheels and shafts was a highly skilled trade with its products correspondingly costly—horses were expensive to breed and feed. Thus the simplest way to move goods to London might have been via Stratford and Oxford. More particularly and summarily; goods going from Whitefriars could have been loaded on the Sherbourne at the Charter House,* passed down the river to its confluence with the Sowe at Whitley, on to Stoneleigh, then down the Avon and on to London via the Stour, by passing Edgehill, and requiring only about forty miles overland to Oxford. It is noteworthy that a few years after Shakespeare's death, Charles I faced his crisis against Parliament by shifting his resources to Oxford, before his army proceeded in the direction of Stratford, encountering parliamentary forces at Edgehill. This shows the way taken by the king; also that to Kenilworth, one of his keypoints. The route to London via Oxford links four other important abbeys: southwards along the Avon at Pershore and Tewkesbury; northwards by the Avon to Stoneleigh, and on through Coventry to Leicester.

The Dissolution of the Monasteries (1536) must have been a traumatic time for those in charge. But also there must have been a faction inside these institutions that secretly welcomed the wind of change. The official Roman church was far away on the continent, and could easily get out of touch with its appointed rulers on the spot, in view of the long journey times taken by couriers. Furthermore, the pressure of population was then very great. Official

*It was itself a monastery dedicated by Richard II to his Queen Anne, during his visit to the North in 1385.

religion looked with horror on any form of artificial birth control. But long before the days of Sigmund Freud, the church had advanced its own method for the sublimation of emotion: the monastic vocation. Whereas, after the scientific revolution started by Copernicus, the young men of Europe increasingly looked to the New World for their inspiration and motivation, the same youths would have formerly sublimated their feelings by working together inside monasteries.

It is inevitable that this escape reinforced the creative drive for dramatic expression. But it is also likely that the correspondingly unimaginative official *Lord's Spiritual* should have looked askance on any liberal expression of emotion. We all know how, even much later in the nineteenth century, the horror of the "crudities" of Shakespeare led to an amended edition prepared by Bowdler; and how he even went on to amend parts of the Bible for the same reasons.

Thus a succession of plays may have been unofficially performed inside monasteries without a word of publicity escaping. Chaucer tells us that some infamies were blanketed by the walls; but infamy always lives in balance with creativity. Indeed, the satellite abbeys of the Middle Ages may have formed the prototype for the later development of universities such as Oxford and Cambridge. When it came to the break-up, there must have been a feeling that some effort towards the salvage of long-considered, well-tried, and contemplated expression ought to be attempted. The search for a runner towards the metropolis of London may then have started. The monks desperately wanted to get their ideas taken up by society. And finally the plan may have involved one: William Shakespeare, from the nearby village of Stratford upon Avon, a place connected with Coventry by a natural, mediaeval river highway. Archaeologists have already found evidence that Bretford and Brandon, villages towards Rugby, were visited by this route.

How much internal evidence is there for these ideas? It is noteworthy that the last historical play is that about Henry VIII, which is quite short and largely portrays the downfall of Cardinal Woolsey, an outstanding event taking place in the first period of the king's reign. Does this last historical effort, which might have originated at a time close to the dissolution of monasteries, signify the end of the series because of its coincidence with the impending demise? Another feature of the plays is their total commitment to the concept of the "three-tier" universe, coupled with the idea that a theatre reflects the universe in miniature. The playhouse where the plays were first publicly presented was called The Globe, which the author also describes as a Wooden O. Much has been written about the homosexual aspects of Shakespeare, particularly the sonnets. We might emphasise that love towards both sexes is a valid subject for sublimation; it is perfectly honourable for a man to express his fellow-feeling towards another male by all kinds of worthy activity.

In support of the thesis here outlined we obviously bring no hitherto unknown positive evidence, but rather an examination of it in the light of recent scientific evolution. The orthodox view that most of Shakespeare was written over a period of ten years from 1594 to 1604, is difficult to accept for the following reasons:

1. Such an output would suppose an unprecedented explosion of creative activity.
2. It leaves a barren period at the end of Shakespeare's life.
3. The Copernican revolution, started before 1543 was overlooked by the author, or treated as though it did not exist.
4. Many stirring events took place after the Dissolution of the Monasteries. The Spanish Armada (1588), the Colonisation of America, the realisation that the world which Shakespeare calls 'The Great Globe itself' was a minor satellite near the sun, the observation by Galileo (1610), that the planet Jupiter held four orbiting moons. All these attested facts are not considered.

The author or authors were clearly disciples of St. Thomas Aquinas. For centuries the latter's synthesis of Greek science with Christian theology formed the Aristotelian basis for Christendom; and it harmonises perfectly with the philosophical background of Shakespeare's drama. Thus in *The Merchant of Venice* where Lorenzo and

Jessica are eloping on a dark night, Lorenzo says: "Look how the floor of heaven is thick inlaid with patines of bright gold." The author again and again compares a person's life with the part of an actor on a stage. The theatrical terms; *Gods* for gallery, and *Pit* for the darkness below, show how the metaphor has become ingrained.

Everyone agrees that the rise of Christendom marked a profound step forward for humanity: kings ruled for the good of everyone and set a tone as we can see in these lines by an anonymous poet:

> The knight fought for all,
> The smith wrought for all,
> The monk thought for all.

Inside monasteries this ethos could have been carried to an even more intense phase. A small group might have emerged to form *la creme de la creme*, leading to the possibility of composite authorship and a unique group marriage of minds.

Thus the values and images of Christendom could have been enshrined to form a bulwark for the Christian way of thinking. Centuries of thought may have been passed down to posterity as a simple "globe" picture of man in his universe. This is still valuable; but it was based on the earthy dimension of length. We have only to elevate it to a higher level, a superglobe, a sphere derived not just from length; but from the very bones of physics itself: mass, space, and time. We hope to describe just how, this idea may be verified in a later chapter.

Chapter 3

The Dead-beat Wave of Time

For men may come and men may go,
But I go on for ever.

—Tennyson

Zeno of Elea (490–430 B.C.) constructed paradoxes, apparently contradictory, about time and space. Achilles chasing a tortoise could never reach it; because by the time he had reached the point where the tortoise originally was, it would have moved on a bit; and by the time he had covered the bit, it would have moved on again; and so on to infinity. As a counterargument the Greek atomists, Epicurus et al, produced the atomic theory. According to this, space was filled by atoms and voids. Thus they seemed to have disproved Zeno; but even so, there was still a difficulty about motion. How could anything move if space was already full of something? Further, how could even Torricelli's vacuum allow any influence—electric, gravitational, or magnetic—to project itself across nothing? To the end of his days, Descartes could not reconcile himself to the idea of a perfect vacuum; hence his suggestion of a *plenum* pervading all space. The term *field* has been adopted by physicists to cover their lack of a reasonable theory. Nevertheless it remains difficult to define space. Even after he purported to have eliminated simultaneity, Einstein spent a long time trying to harmonise *field* with thermodynamics.

One of the salient realisations of nineteenth century thermodynamics was that time moves one way—forward. According to the second law of thermodynamics, heat always drains away from the body hotter than its surroundings to give a lower temperature. This discovery made the leaders of the day very pessimistic. H. G. Wells described space as "That immense void, in which all light, and life, and being was but the thin and vanishing splendour of a falling star." Sir James Jeans thought physics to be "altogether more important than biology." Bertrand Russell said, "There can be no escape from the second law of thermodynamics."

A recent issue of *Discovery* (February 1987) describes how seven ineluctable arrows all point to a one-way direction for time. To the average person these seem like glimpses of the obvious. But modern physics seems unable to find any reason why time should not flow backwards as well as forwards. Newtonian physics, on the other hand, looks at the universe with common sense. Newton's definition of time describes it as a flow, and proves that he thought time must inevitably move forward—a river never flows uphill. This is another cogent reason for reversion to Newtonian principles; he had at least got his feet on the ground. But physics, misled by Relativity, is now standing on its head.

First let us define the adjective *dead-beat*, and see exactly how it describes the "one-way" progression of time. Encyclopedias and elementary textbooks of physics don't say much about dead-beat waves. But there are some examples found in nature; and they exemplify one of the two basic types of wave-motion: there are harmonic waves and dead-beat waves. Just as you find the usual harmonic wave-forms on the sea, so you may find *tsunamis* ariving from underwater earth tremors. There are also tidal bores that travel along tapering estuaries. It is certainly worth going to Stonebench in Gloucestershire to see the Severn bore, especially if there happens to be a southwesterly wind. Another example of a dead-beat wave is the piling up of air on the leading edge of a supersonic plane. Perhaps the classical examples of dead-beat action are to be found in the functioning of oil-filled shock-absorbers, and the rubber pivots bearing car engines.

There is also an elegant demonstration that anyone can do in the lab. Using sodium thiosulphate, common photographer's "hypo," you can easily make a supersaturated solution of salt, and then allow it to cool to room temperature. Now simply drop in a minute crystal of "hypo" into the supersaturated solution, and you will see a dead-beat crystallisation wave of almost explosive speed and violence. You get a model of creation and the passage of time in microcosm.

25

In fact all explosions produce dead-beat waves. The big bang was no exception, and we shall see how everything that happens in life depends upon it. After the big bang, what was as thick as mud became clearer than perspex. Future time was exactly nothing, a perfect vacuum; everybody was living at the leading edge of time. And this solved the age-old problem of motion, which so worried Zeno and the ancient Greeks. Dead-beat time is forever moving on through nothing, and the present is being instantaneously recreated. As Newton demonstrated, movement presupposes acceleration; and acceleration may only be achieved by the exercise of will and strength of mind.*

What is further entailed by dead-beat time? Even an explosion has to be backed by something; usually the released spent gases. But we have to think of something much more subtle for time. We may believe that a swarm of ultimate particles—electrons, protons, neutrons, and neutrinos, were released with the big bang. The last of these shows no appreciable mass, and is very hard to detect. A neutrino may be taken to be the smallest unit of space and time which can exist alone. And we believe that the immense spaces between stars and galaxies are filled with inert neutrinos. We shall see later how the extraordinary proportion of energy associated with massive particles fits in perfectly with time moving on at the speed of light.

Another strange feature of any dead-beat wave is its capacity to add a dimension. Take for example the river Severn. As its bore approaches it instantaneously lifts the level of the Severn upwards, at right angles to the surface of the river. In the same sort of way, when the leading edge of time approaches, it gives us all an extra depth. Any past event lives on in space/time, having gained an extra degree of freedom. Most people imagine that the old phrase "everlasting life" entailed a connotation of extreme boredom. Actually the phrase originally meant "all-embracing life," an expansion of the mind to give a feeling of being in tune with all existence. There is only one rule that we should rightly know: it is to live our lives so that they each make up a consistent whole, an integrated pattern.

*See page 2, par. 3 of Introduction.

From birth to death we ought to be trying to crystallize our minds into some final symmetrical order.

How may we check dead-beat time against careful experience? We are all quite certain that the nearest objects to the planet Earth are set at extraordinarily great distances away in space. These big figures have actually given rise to a new adjective—*astronomical*. Everyone rather takes these findings for granted, but it is only in comparatively recent times that even the distance of the moon became known with any accuracy. Thus when Newton first conceived the idea of universal gravitation, it became clear to him that the moon should be ever engaged in a process of falling down to Earth as a result of the mutual attractions of the two bodies. The only thing that kept the moon circling was its original angular momentum. And because he had discovered the mathematical relation between momentum and force—his second law—he realised that the opposed gravitational and centrifugal forces must be in balance. At first theoretical calculation did not agree with experiemental observation. But about that time, a more accurate estimate of the distance of the moon was published, and the new data then agreed precisely.

The clarification, however, did produce a great puzzle; which has not yet been resolved even to this day. It concerned the reason for both Earth and moon, and indeed for all the planets and satellites of the solar system, having the correct angular velocities to keep them all permanently in circulation. The question was put to Newton, and he could only say that the Creator must have given them all exactly the right "shoves." Later, a French nobleman, Count Laplace, thought he had the answer: the Solar System must have condensed from an extensive nebula. We recall his famous boast to Napoleon: "My system has no need for a creator!" And indeed most people think that the Earth simply arose from a nebula. But in fact, the theory is untenable. It does not conform to the law of conservation of angular momentum. If the solar system had indeed been condensed from a nebula, with the angular velocities of the planets indicating the degree of nebula spin, then the sun itself should have been flattened to an oblate disc! This is where dead-beat time demands some modification of the nebular theory, which might modify it to fill the gap.

According to dead-beat time, all the celestial bodies in the universe have been equally in pro-rata expansion since the big bang. We have to believe that the first explosion of the big bang, was soon followed by a swarm of almost simultaneous lesser explosions. In this way fragments of the original primeval atom were each widely scattered, before they themselves individually exploded, to form separate less extensive clouds. These lesser clouds were the precursors of the multitudinous individual stars that make up each galaxy. The original galaxial clouds were so far apart, and the directions of the recessions so skew, that they were later easily detected by their respective red shifts. On the other hand, the matter forming individual stellar clouds was proportionally so close, that it came under the countervailing influence of gravity. This in turn induced an angular acceleration which led on, by the natural conservation of angular momentum, to enhanced spins. The high degree of spin and the consequential oblation of the stellar parents then led further to the separation of ringlike belts around and away from central suns. Because of the countereffect of gravitation and the smallness of the angles of divergence, the corresponding recession from the original centre of the big bang has been difficult to detect. But this influence could well modify the original nebula theory sufficiently to make it highly probable.

A few months before World War Two, we spent two weeks not far from Ventnor, Isle of Wight. Looking east from high ground towards Sandown, a few miles away, we heard the sound of naval guns at practice. One could see a flash of light and then hear the thud of an explosion nearly a minute later. You get a similar effect in a thunderstorm: a flash and then a peal of thunder. This experience reminds us of the wave origins of both light and sound; light, of course, being the most rapid. It also distinguishes between dead-beat and harmonic origins. Flashes arrive as a crescendo and smoothly die away; but the cacophonous noise of an explosion contrasts sharply with the harmonic light. An even better analogy for the big bang can be seen in any fireworks display. These usually include the firing of high-altitude rockets that explode at a predetermined height, giving an early flash and a retarded bang. This initial bang separates its primal charge into sub units. These are timed to individually explode slightly later to give a shower of stars. This sequence may closely describe the train of events after the cosmic big bang. Thus the primeval atom became separated into a number of material fractions, and then each of these later further exploded to give a series of immense clouds—the precursors of the individual galaxies seen today. How does this description fit in with actual observation? The photographs of disseminated galaxies shows them as oblated spheroids. Further the oblations have axes pointing in all directions. This is in remarkable harmony with all the closer celestial objects of the solar system. The sun and all its planets are oblated in the same direction as the Milky Way.

Thus we see how there is quite a bit of directly observable evidence in favour of the big bang theory; although this theory had languished and had long been out of favour. Another indication of the violent origins of the cosmos is shown by the frequency of pockmarked craters on the surfaces of the moon and other solar satellites.

It is very instructive to read what Fred Hoyle has to say about the well-observed slowness of rotation of the sun,* compared with what it ought to be to conform with orthodox nebula theory about the sun's origin. After spending nine pages on all the difficulties attending the Laplace idea, he puts forward the preposterous notion that the sun lost its spin by loss of hydrogen amounting to all the planets of the solar system put together. He further admits that the Sun must have lost its spin, late on during its condensation from gas. But the prime objection to the loss of such a lot of hydrogen, is how did it come to condense into the Sun in the first place? To explain the escape of the planets, he invokes the force of magnetism. In many people's minds, magnetism is closely allied with electricity. But it must be emphasized that magnetism is only

---

*__Solar Rotation.__ What rotates at this rate is the equatorial part of the visible, surface layer of the Sun. This is all we can observe. Astro-physicists have, however, formulated various theories about what happens inside. _Some Facts_ In 1968 the rotation rate of the Sun varied between 11.7 and 14.9 degrees per day over a period of only 12 weeks. In 1972 it rose to 15.3 degrees per day for a short period.

Reference: __Robert Howard,__ "The Rotation of the Sun," _Scientific American_, April 1975, 106–14.

secondary to electric force. This is because the latter always occurs in nature as tangible electrons. They are fundamental to the physical world, and it is only by their motion that magnetism comes into being. Magnetism certainly plays a rather larger role in science, particularly in chemistry than was once thought. These days it clarifies just how two electrons, which are supposed to repel one another at short distance, can nevertheless get together to form a co-valent bond, so essential to organic chemistry. But the idea that magnetism can shift a mass of nonmagnetic hydrogen three thousand times the size of the earth across the depths of space is hard to imagine.

We can perhaps best understand how the planets of the solar system expanded away from the sun by thinking of an old-fashioned spherical Christmas pudding full of raisins and currants. On cooking, we may expect the pudding to expand. But two currants originally close together, will only diverge microscopically, whereas a couple, originally separated by a radius or more, will drift apart by inches. Surely, anyone must see the true deduction: the plain, simple, and straightforward view that the planets got away by the general, far-flung expansion of the universe. There are, however, a few outstanding, special indications in favour of dead-beat time and general expansion at the speed of light.

The Spiral Arms of Galaxies

Although the galaxies behave as though they were enormously expanded satellite systems, we should remember that they are so extensive that they may have only revolved about twenty times during their complete existence. Whereas, supposing the galaxies were rotating under the influence of gravity alone, stars near the centre should be rotating at a higher speed. The picture actually found suggests that some other force has taken charge to overcome gravity and accelerate the outermost members, thus producing spirals.

The Olber (1758–1840) Paradox

This arises from the obvious consideration that the night sky ought to be white instead of black. If, as seems incontrovertible, there are a hundred thousand million stars in our own galaxy, and further a similar number in every galactic nebula outside, as well as the realisation that this type of nebula is to be found all over the sky, then we ought to find light arriving from every direction. And this should produce a uniform white background. This darkness is all the more remarkable, since it has been found that the lines of time and space are bent towards centres of gravitation. There must be some very fundamental reason why star light is so faint. This could be explained by thinking that all stellar objects may be in a process of recession at a very high speed—the speed of light. Nearer objects may be correspondingly more prominent because their proximity markedly reduces their apparent recessions and makes these objects seem relatively brighter when viewed from earth.

A Simplification of the Fitzgerald Contraction

Fitzgerald discovered that fast-moving objects were contracted in the directions of their motions according to a simple formula, which arises from the ultimate nature of the velocity of light, C. Any distance, x, is always equal to $C\,t$, where t is the corresponding time taken by a light signal to cover x. This means that C is a steady characteristic of space/time, similar to the velocity of sound in air or any other medium. In fact C was a limiting velocity, so that if a transverse high speed, say v, were applied to an object already travelling at C, the resultant was not $\sqrt{C^2 + v^2}$, as might have been expected from Pythagoras, but still just C, although the direction of the resultant would remain along the expected hypoteneuse. This means that the length of the object had to suffer a contraction in the ratio: $1 : \dfrac{\sqrt{C^2 - v^2}}{C}$

(see Figure 1).

A length OA, velocity v, becomes contracted to OB, because the predicted resultant, $\sqrt{C^2 + v^2}$, OD, can never be greater than OE, C. Since triangles ▲OAD and ▲OBE are similar:

$$\frac{OB}{OA} = \frac{BE}{AD} = \frac{\sqrt{C^2 - v^2}}{C} \text{ or } \sqrt{1 - (v^2/C^2)}$$

The Fitzgerald contraction is a result that Einstein fudges in *Relativity*.* This contraction is the basis for special relativity and leads algebraically to the well-known mass/energy relation (see chapter 12).

Fitzgerald via Bradley

According to special relativity, any one framework of reference is as good as any other. So that the Fitzgerald contraction may be very simply deduced, use the principle of Bradley's aberration (1727). An observer at A, in a spaceship SS (see Figure 2), moving close to Earth with velocity v, comparable with that of light, C, records the aberration BB' of a distant high light signal. This originates at B, B'B being equal to AD, where D is a point directly beneath the signal on Earth. The triangle ABD may now be regarded as a triangle of velocities, with BD representing C, AD, v, and AB, $\sqrt{C^2 + V^2}$. This would presuppose that the two velocities behaved in accordance with classical mechanics and supplemented one another in the usual way. But because the velocity of light, C, is limited to C, the hypotenuese, AB, must be reduced to AE, where AE defines C. The perpendicular, EF, thus becomes equal to $\sqrt{C^2 - v^2}$, and AF becomes v, AE becoming C. Thus any length AD on earth has to be reduced in the spaceship, by the fraction:

$$\frac{\sqrt{(C^2 - v^2)}}{C} \text{ or } \sqrt{1 - (v^2/C^2)} :$$

*Albert Einstein, *Relativity* (London: University Paperbacks, Methuen and Co. Ltd., 1920), appendix 1, p. 115.

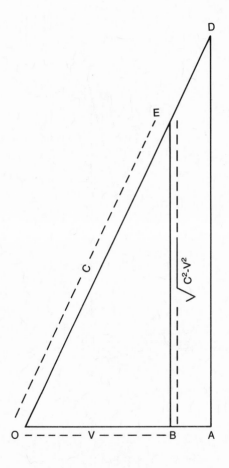

Figure 1. Contraction Due to Speed

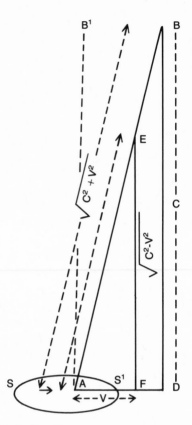

Figure 2. Contraction by Bradley

the Fitzgerald contraction, as before. Of course, time inside the spaceship must also suffer a corresponding modification. The Fitzgerald contraction is the basis for Einstein's special relativity, and leads on algebraically to the well-known equation : $E = mC^2$.

In Chapter 5, "Calculating the Gravitational Constant," the very low potential of gravity relative to electricity (1: 1.25×10^{36}) is shown to agree with the slight curvature of space/time (1 : 1.24×10^{36}) found by taking expansion from the big bang to be at velocity C. Thus we see how astronomy itself completes the unification of the physical world.

Of course, the relativity principle that holds that any one frame of reference is as good as another does not hold true in practice. Otherwise we might still expect the sun to skip round the Earth at 600 million miles per day, a result quite inconsistent with gravitation.

Finally, telescopes have recently disclosed the existence of very massive and dense objects, at the greatest depths in space. These precursors of galaxies are radiating energy at an enormous rate, and they also disclose another peculiar effect: a double image. This may mean that their light is refracted around two sides of a dense primal universe. The dead-beat wave of time is indeed a flow—it is really a very refreshing river.

Chapter 4

The Evolution of
Arts and Sciences

A rose that blooms once, blooms for ever.
—J. W. Dunne

What do Shakespeare and Newton have in common? They both gathered together fragments and produced foundations. Thus before Shakespeare there was a series of primitive, medieval efforts designed to make deep ethical impressions—the morality plays. These also give hints of cloistered origins. But with Shakespeare, as well as other Elizabethans, there was a sustained enlargement embracing hitherto undreamt of vistas: a springlike blossoming of culture. After Shakespeare there came a flatter, more formal period, when literature became fettered with a growth of man-made arid rules. This was followed by a romantic revival near the end of the eighteenth century and the advent of the French and American Revolutions.

Newtonian mechanics was followed by a similar flat sequence, where it lost some of its impetus, during the later eighteenth century. The dry rules of two-dimensinal geometry took over from the more expansive, yet all-embracing and more stimulating concepts of Newton. It may be that the time is soon coming for a renewed outbreak. Both Shakespeare and Newton produced exciting new pictures of the world for everyone to share.

We all ought to have a working picture of the world outside of ourselves. This is basic to culture and human endeavour in every field. We should also try to find a plausible balance between our efforts to achieve something, and to give up something in return—to lay our "brick." Ideally and naturally, this working picture of ourselves within a larger world ought to fire us with zest and positive endeavour, but unfortunately there seem to be more and more people, who for some reason fail to achieve this desirable frame of mind and, therefore, they cannot open themselves up into a flatout drive in any direction. This unhappiness has come about primarily because they have adopted an incorrect interpretation of the physical world. Years ago the picture was delightfully straightforward and simple: the extensive flat surface of the world lay under a huge dome, the firmament, with an overhanging highest gallery, "the gods," and below an indescribably offensive "pit," a very blown-up and much magnified theatre. Those then on the stage were mostly either villains or heroes. Today everything has become surrealistic. The truth is that everyone then thought that they had a firm and direct experience of the great theatre and of their own precise role in a preordained living drama. But the vision has been shattered, because they have suddenly come to realise that the physical world seems not at all consistent with the old-fashioned dream. We said "suddenly" because all speeds are relative, and the term is applied in relation to the grooved habits humanity has acquired over many centuries.

The rise of science is comparatively very recent; yet enough time has elapsed to show that basic feelings have seeped down into the general subconsciousness of society and profoundly modified its total infrastructure. For example—Newtonian dynamics was applied first to ballistics. The drilling of cannons led on to the perfection of steam cylinders. Steam engines introduced the Industrial Revolution. Dynamics merged into thermodynamics, and its main finding, the reality of ultimate particles of matter, became established. To the average man the Age of Science achieved its miracles mainly from the novel uses of electricity—radio, TV, et cetera. Early science invigorated and galvanised society precisely because it was able to present an alternative, up-to-date, yet still sharply focussed picture of the physical world. The simple idea that every particle of matter attracted every other particle was easy to grasp, and it conveyed a feeling of unity. Later the need for a medium to transmit electric, magnetic, and gravitational forces across empty space gave intimations of an all-pervading ocean, the "luminiferous ether." This was also a clear-cut notion that later reflected the spiritualism of some nineteenth century scientists.

But with the twentieth century there appeared theories that only experts could attempt to either interpret or understand. Yet the authority of science had become so great, its predictions and physical achievements so impressive, that everyone looked up to it as the one fount of certain knowledge. Descartes believed that mathematics could solve all the problems of science; and the development of coordinate geometry into vector analysis culminated with the two present foremost theories of physics: relativity and quantum mechanics. At the same time, all that relativity could offer the common man was the notion that any one frame of reference was as good as any other, that there was apparently no single or ultimate foundation to existence. Similarly, quantum mechanics mysteriously pronounced that material particles could only be described as waves of probability.

When people looked outside themselves and found nothing tangible nor bedrock, they naturally switched their attention inwards, so that they found justification for self-centredness, and the whole coherence of society began to be undermined. Therefore, the only single and simple thing that could restore the balance is the rediscovery of a clear-cut picture; something that could become and might provide a sheet-anchor preventing any further drift to chaos.

Why then did relativity fail to generate a picture? It springs from elaborate deduction, not from direct experiment. To discriminate between these, we might think of the ratio between the diameter and circumference of a circle, π. The constancy of π may be found by measurement or mathematics. The traditional way is best because of everyday experience. The constancy of the velocity of light came long before relativity. The latter ignored Descartes's original, triple rectilinear frame, and concentrated on just two axes: space and time. Thus Professor Eddington says: "The space/time frame is fictitious and arbitrary, overlaid on the world like lines of latitude and longitude." It is clearly right to suppose that time lapses at right angles to space, otherwise any array of stationary objects might change their positions without moving. What is not logical is to suppose that the variability of space/time alone determines the play of events. This is a relic of mechanistic eighteenth century thinking.

When a body is cooled to near absolute zero, its heat energy, i.e., the movement of its ultimate particles, does not smoothly drain away, as might be supposed, but rather it does so by little jumps, a series of critical and random fits and starts. We are familiar with this when we see or hear the movement of a Geiger counter near a source of radiation; or when we notice random flecks on a TV screen. But we are even more aware of the way a beaker of water reaches boiling point. As the water gets near boiling, minute bubbles appear randomly here and there. Conversely, should the warming cease, the bubbles gradually decrease and die away until the water again becomes still and clear. The draining away of energy near zero follows a similar course. This means that energy is particulate, that it exists as indivisible, ultimate units. If energy, which may easily be shown to compose the play of three ultimate dimensions—mass, length, and time—is particulate, then each of its three fundamentals should also be so.

First consider mass: if there are indivisible units of energy—quanta: 6.6×10^{-27} erg secs, then, according to mass/energy, there must be indivisible units of mass—ca: 5.9×10^{-46} gm. This extremely small quantity represents the smallest particle in the universe; it turns out to be vastly smaller than a hydrogen atom (1.67×10^{-24} gm), or even an electron (9×10^{-28} gm). But if there are indivisible units of mass, there must be indivisible zones of space/time containing those masses. These fundamental considerations have a very important bearing on conditions in "Flatland."

Why There Can Be No Curves in "Flatland"

As soon as relativity became a vogue theory, efforts were naturally made to popularise its ideas, and so an analogy with "Flatland" was introduced. It was particularly useful in explaining the curvature of the space/time continuum, said to be responsible for gravitation. If a Flatlander wanted to go from A to B, and there was a hill in between, he would be inclined to walk round the hill without noticing it because he would have no sense or appreciation of going up or down. We all fall into this sort of delusion when we go around the apparently flat surface of the world. The significance of "Flatland" arises because Cartesian analysis has become a "Flatland" exercise. It developed first from conic sections: simple curves for circle, parabola, and hyperbola, with their corresponding algebraic equations. We have to go right back to Joseph Louis Lagrange (1737—1815), who first disregarded the third axis of his great compatriot, Descartes. Newton has already achieved algebraic expression for his axioms as equations of motion. Lagrange went on to clarify by treating them as being reducible to the surface of a graph whose axes were space and time. He thus became the true discoverer of "Flatland." Analysis extended its rules in harmony with the development of algebra.

These rules are very like the grammar and syntax of a language. Reality was seen as a page, of which the edges were space and time. For example, the Irishman W. R. Hamilton, realised in 1850 that there might be something imagined as being outside the page of space and time. Thus he enlarged the rules of calculus: when the equation of a line is integrated in analytical terms, it amounts to a summation of the area between the line and its parameter so that a unidimensional quantity becomes two-dimensional. Conversely differentiation shrinks an area into a line. Thus there could be any number of imaginary directions outside the page; but these could only exist in the minds of analysts.

This imagery led on to the invention of new symbols, again according to the rules of analysis. It was as though archeologists, not content with translating the hieroglyphics of the Rosetta stone, went on to imagine new signs not actually on the stone, but which yet conformed to rules for real symbols. In this way mathematics, which Galileo called "the handmaid of science" advanced to the "language of science." But language always induces pedantry and breeds ossification. Latin once stiffened Aristotle into a tyranny that needed a Reformation to undo. Today a new tyranny has led to another crisis. Analysis parts company from experiment when we approach ultimate movement. It carries on as though there were no finite limits; as though it were doing an exercise in calculus. All motion would become the combined resultant of a large number of infinitesimal rectilinear movements. In "Flatland," there are only two dimensions, so the texture of its surface must be made up of a multitude of minute squares. It is impossible to break these down into the infinitesimal units necessary to arrive at the formula: $x = w^2r$ (x = angular acceleration, w = the angular velocity, and r = the radius of the system). It thus appears that "Flatlanders" should move like chessmen, a step or steps forward or along the rank. There would be no possibility of turning, because there would be no third dimension about which to turn. On the other hand it seems clear that any real three-dimensional particle must have six fundamentally separate degrees of freedom: the option of moving along, or around the three separate dimensions of space.

The finding that energy is particulate is so important that we should consider its thermal origin in more detail. The nineteenth century has already demonstrated that heat is really the combined movements, straight or rotary, of atoms or electrons. As a lump of solid matter cools, it first loses its tendency to move striaght, because each unit is electrically connected in a tight crystal lattice; and its energy is rapidly communicated. Thus we may consider energy dissipation within single atoms, even down to single electrons. We should also assume that electrons are able to gyrate freely about their respective axes. When their straight and circling motions become less frequent near zero temperature, there may come a time when these are reduced to single spasmodic jerks—the electron does a single lap; it sends out a quantum of radiant energy; then it resumes quiescence. Because the quantum takes up a waveform, we reach the surprising inference that rotary and straight motions remain separate and individual to the bitter end.

This fundamental dissonance between orthodox mathematics and experimental science lies at the root of the problem of restoring a simple picture of the world so that everyone may be happy again. So long as as we are trying to cram into two dimensions what properly belongs to three, we are trying, vainly, to square a circle; we have become captives of "Flatland." How then can experiment alone reconstruct a simple, yet credible picture of the world and of our own individual role in it? We have to think of the smallest and simplest particle, the radiant quantum, the photon. We saw how this slight unit, weighing only about 10^{-45} gm, could be in parity with straight and angular motion. Because it may spin and translate at the same rate, its energy becomes the product of its mass and the square of that speed, MC^2, in agreement with mass/energy and the expansion of the universe. The increasing recession of the more distant nebulae points to wave emanation from a focal point ca.: 2×10^{-10} years ago; and this figure also fits the experimentally found, yet minuscule gravitational constant (6.7 $\times 10^{-8}$ dyne cm^2 gm^2); not at all easily reconciled with either quantum or relativity physics (see Chapter 5). How can the particles of inert matter be moving as waves, both in a circle and in a straight line, to register their prodigious energy? How can a quiescent outer electron still retain its mass, while doing an extra lap to generate a quantum in space/time? The answer comes from a forgotten, third, fundamental dimension.

Potential Energy

The third dimension, "being," is necessary to clarify potential energy. It takes the place of "field" in orthodox physics. The propagation of waves requires a rhythmic alternation between kinetic and potential energy, and we may believe that the latter is built up from being time and length, BL^2T^{-2}, just as kinetic energy arises from mass, time, and length, ML^2T^{-2}. The elusiveness and unpredictability of the electron emphasises the continuous flux between its positions in space and being. In fact this third fundamental dimension may be simply and economically the long-known quality of mass seen from a vector aspect; just as until recently, time was not taken to have a length as well as a temporal aspect. We know that a third type of extension exists, because you can't make a simple cross without defining a triple cross—you can't have a signpost without a supporting prop, or a weathercock without a spire. In analytical terms, the X and Y axes of a Cartesian frame are only completed by the addition of a transverse Z axis, being the hidden axis of mass.

We are often called to agree to the time and place of the next meeting. This data is clearly similar to that in a timetable, a programme, or even Eddington's arbitrary lines of latitude and longitude. It forms a possible framework for future events, but the actual events remain unpredictable, and their expectation forms one of the main incentives and charms of living. Time and place are only the scaffolding that outlines the possibilities for creation in the present. We should remember that all the many physicochemical and biological intricacies of this creation may be in the course of duplication in time and being. The passage of time may quite simply be just adding a dimension, with all the freedom that this entails. Thus we ought to distinguish sharply between a two- and a three-dimensionally defined event. Neither relativity nor quantum physics makes any attempt to define that narrow section of time we call "now." We saw in Chapter 3 how they both envisaged past, present, and future merging together into a single block. Alternatively we believe that the present is simply the spatial and temporal boundary formed by the dead-beat wave of time in its surge from the big bang about twenty billion years ago. On this boundary we are conceived, born, grown, and finally weave together our completed personality so that everything that has been, is, or will be, is finally captured and permanently preserved.

When radiation emanates from a focal point, it proceeds similarly to a series of expanding spherical surfaces—shells. The curvature of these shells gets less and less, inversely as their radii increase. It is the old picture of a stone thrown in a pond. Thus the slight curvature of space/time is responsible for gravity (see Chapter 5). In this way, we have come to the restoration and revival of a vivid world scene, conceivable even by a child. First there is the central, focal point, about 20 billion years ago, from which the whole material cosmos creatively expanded. Next, this radiation, like rays from the sun, shines out transversely and transcendently on all sides, activating and creating the slightly curved plane of space and time we know as the present. We are back on a stage; we have a part; we have to fit in with others on the stage; we know exactly where we are going and what we are doing; what we are about to achieve; and what are our next activities in order of priorities. Above all we know that whatever we do is being recorded and captured for ever. In contrast to our new freedom, we remember just how offensively prescribed were the inhabitants of two-dimensional "Flatland," beside which the Gulag Archipelago would be a playground. And we saw how, in passing from two- to three-dimensions, freedom had expanded to give four surprising fresh possibilities. This we may expect when our lives are wholly completed.

We began by seeing the world allegorically as a theatre, but we might have moved nearer to reality by seeing our world view as being like that of a member of an evolving dramatic group. First came the "Little Earth Society," as symbolised by Shakespeare. This began in a simple way, yet achieved great success. The majority enjoyed their parts and found a happy self-expression. Some thought their society marvellous; their plays were perfect, the plots wonderful, any idea of change would be anathema.

Then there came a period of transition, when it was gradually realised that their stage was, after all, too small, their premises cramped, the plays stale and predictable, the plots too simple and obvious. This change in feeling caused great strain and stress, leading to cross-purposes, feuds, and conflict. Finally, the majority settled for reconstruction on a much more ambitious scale. They changed their name to "The Solar Theatre," symbolised by the ideas of Newton. After a long period of adjustment and crosscurrents, calm was restored. Most players began to wonder how anyone was ever content to put up with all the restrictions and frustrations of the "Little Earth Society."

But even the emancipated Solar Theatre eventually came under criticism. It seemed, almost imperceptibly, to be losing coherence. The very foundations became suspect, and the stage, the central focus of any theatre, began to disintegrate, becoming less and less well-defined. The plays, too, became shapeless. All that the players could do was to perfect their skill in conversation and in their expression of feeling. To compensate for lack of plot, action had to be stepped up to the limit to give an abundance of noise

44

and animation. Some began to wonder whether the theatre had not degenerated into a madhouse with no real objective at all.

And so there began an even further movement to again reform the society on more rational lines. Ideally they must move forward and effect sharp innovation, but at the same time, the theatre should retrieve some of its original coherence. Broadly, reformers were in favour of the utmost individuality, combined with the retention of a sense of belonging to a creativity outside themselves; in keeping with the perfect symmetry of the larger and more embracing theatre they had in mind. This might be known as the "Ad-lib Theatre," because everyone should feel free to follow his or her own self-expression and not be forced into a mould prescribed by someone else. Yet because each player should have a rough outline of what the whole play was about, a working plan, he would be able to conform to its spirit. And since he would be aware that his playing was being recorded, he would have less fear of what other players might think of his efforts. If the society claimed to be alive, then it must evolve and grow, just as had happened before in its long history.

Chapter 5

The Experimental Verification of Dead-beat Time

When the loose mountain trembles from on high,
Shall gravitation cease if you go by?
—Alexander Pope

Our little lives are bounded by a spell.
—Shakespeare

Any idea, innovation, or hypothesis worth considering, ought to offer the possibility of verification. In science, it ought to fit together with other quite independently observed results. This is especially important concerning the wave of time. Any new view ought to point the way to a further economy of ideas. The wave of time idea shows up hitherto unnoticed resemblances between surface tension and gravitation. What are the similarities between these apparently quite separate and distinct physical forces? Both show relatively weak indications of their existence, and both act positively as separate forms of attraction. There was a hundred years' gap between the concept of universal gravitation and the actual measurement of its potential by Cavendish; and the total force of attraction between two one-gram masses, one centimeter apart, turned out to be only 6.67×10^{-8} dyne. Surface tension was first associated with the kinetic theory of molecules, when it was noticed that molecular attraction generated the appearance of a kind of skin or membrane over individual drops of liquids. Here again the surface tension of water, which incidentally is a very polar and dissociating liquid, amounted to only 74 dynes per cm.

Both Eddington and Dirac attempted to compare gravity with

electricity.* They concentrated on the respective forces acting between an electron and a proton. Unfortunately we have no guarantee that the mass they assigned to an electron is gravitational. It has always been tacitly assumed that the gravitational mass is equivalent to the inertial mass as found experimentally by J. J. Thompson. But the electron is well known to show a fair degree of spin. This and its unpredictability, make it an unsuitable model for the evaluation of gravity. The doubt is eliminated by comparing, not the attraction between electron and proton, but the repulsion between the two protons associated together in a hydrogen molecule. In this way it can be shown that electric force is about 1.25×10^{36} times stronger than the comparable gravitational force (about two thousand times less than Dirac's estimate).†

The expanding universe was first likened by Jeans to an expanding soap bubble. Let us pursue this analogy, and consider surface tension, particularly the way it comes into play. The molecular surface of a drop of water is contained spherically by the fine polar attraction of hydrogen bonding: the residual affinity left over after the main valences of the constituent oxygen and hydrogen atoms have been satisfied. Similar considerations apply to the physical universe. Every one of its atoms is precisely a combination of positive and negative to give many clusters of dipoles. It is remarkable how orthodox physicists are somewhat touchy about residual affinity. According to their account, residual affinity should not exist, because electrons are always engaged in forming inert gas structures that should contain either two, eight, or eighteen electrons, according to the respective sizes of atomic domains. The whole idea seems ridiculous, because the simplest atom, hydrogen, has a bulk greater than the most complex—uranium.

Perhaps the most famous example of the verification principle

"The Physicist's Conception of Nature: Papers in Honor of P. A. M. Dirac" (1973), Ed Mehra.

†The electric repulsion between two protons equals e^2/d^2 dynes, where e is the charge on an electron or proton, and d the distance apart in cm, giving 23×10^{-20} dynes, when $d = 1$ cm. Similarly the gravitational attraction between two protons equals $M^2 K$, d^2 dynes, where M is the mass of a proton, K the gravitational constant, and d, 1 cm, as before. When the electric repulsion factor, e^2 is divided by the gravitational, $M^2 K$, we get the above dimensionless number 1.25×10^{36} times.

is Newton's calculation of the orbit and period of the moon, using the observed acceleration due to gravity on the earth's surface. The agreement between predicted and observed values was of tremendous significance because it became clear that the tendency for material objects to fall extended far away from the earth, whereas before the Age of Science, bodies were supposed to fall because their "earthiness" drove them towards the centre of the earth, then the centre of the universe. Thus Newton's calculation completed a great intellectual revolution, which broadened and liberated the mind with a majestic expansion, and at the same time achieved an extensive economy of ideas. This original revolution is still effective, even in the present day, deep probing of space. A proper verification of the expanding hypersphere, therefore assumes an added importance, because it, too, could initiate quite a new way of thinking about the deeper problems of existence and at the same time complete Newton's vision of universal gravitation.

In fact the two verifications have followed a similar pattern. Thus some years before Newton published his results, he had already formulated his hypothesis, but because the then accepted radius of the moon's orbit did not properly fit his other observations, he reserved his exposition. Later, a closer value was established, which fitted in comfortably with gravitational theory. Incidentally the writer first heard about the expansion of the universe in 1930, when Sir James Jeans published his *Mysterious Universe*, where he gave the past-time back to the focal point of expansion as 2×10^9 years. Later Fred Hoyle, a leading exponent of the rival "continuous-creation" theory, gave a figure nearer 7×10^9 years, or even 9×10^9 years. The author's *Science Is Too Small* (1961) adopted 10^{10} years. Finally the best present value, from the general echo of the big bang is about 2×10^{10} years. General Relativity supposed that space and time might fold back on themselves. In this way spatial and temporal lines could be imagined as being similar to lines of latitude and longitude that circle the earth. If this is so, then the period back to the original great explosion, Hubble's constant, may be considered as the radius of the universe, really a hyperuniverse, because it embraces time as well as space in an unscrambleable melange. Expanding hyperspheric theory sees this radius as constantly increasing in conformity with the expansion of the universe. But with the lapse of time, it has become clear that not only are the extragalactic nebulae receding at speeds proportional to their distances from the Earth, and that their recession points to a definite focal point in the past, but that the farthest galaxies are receding at such high speeds as to indicate a limiting velocity, C—that of light itself. This view leads us to think that all the matter in the universe was once confined to a space of atomic size, forming what has become known as the primeval atom. It suggests that there must have then been in operation a very powerful force able to restrain electricity: primeval gravity. How may we reasonably estimate this enhanced gravity?

We repeat, the expanding universe also shows similarities with a bulging soap bubble by conforming to the laws of surface tension. The surface of a drop of water is held together by a membranelike fabric of water molecules. These are attracted to each other by the residual affinity left over after the main valences of the oxygen and hydrogen of the water have been satisfied. Very similar forces are at work in the material world as a whole. Every one of its atoms is similarly a precise combination of positive and negative electrical attractions or dipoles. In this way the multitudinous dipoles of the planet Earth work together to result in terrestrial gravitation. Similarly both the sun and stars produce solar and stellar gravitation. Under the intense pressure of the dead-beat wave all these dipoles combine together to give a fleeting three-dimensional surface. All real objects are four-dimensional. Figures having only one, two, or three dimensions are only figments of human imagination. An instantaneous cube does not exist in its own right. How then may what was once four-dimensional be suddenly transformed and reduced in extension to only three? It follows directly on from the Fitzgerald contraction as explained in Chapter 3. The prototypes of space/time are four-dimensional, but when its constituent particles, neutrinos, are subject to dead-beat time, they may be condensed and compressed into three. The process may be somewhat similar to the backing of molecules of air on the leading edge of a supersonic plane. This explains why the present tense is always so powerful. Just as the velocity of sound is critical for sound waves, so the velocity of light may be critical for time. Each atomic particle could have begun with four freedoms as a tetrapolar microhyper-

49

sphere. Then it may have momentarily lost one direction of being to become a dipolar sphere. In this way the temporal quality of all existence and material being could have been set up. We saw in the introduction how Rayleigh's and Stefan's relation between temperature and radiation: $E = K t^4$, demanded fourth power expression. This led straight on to the idea of electrons with four degrees of freedom as an electron "gas": giving four alternative paths for kinetic energy.

What extraordinary transformation took place at the big bang? It may have been some transcendant advent of energy as fundamental particles: microhyperspheres, neutrinos, call them what you will. The explosion liberated its unique dead-beat wave, as per all explosions. It characteristically expanded along all four dimensions. But as it proceeded, each minute zone became reduced to three. Tetrahedra became momentarily cubic; hyperspheres turned to spheres; tetrapoles to dipoles; and the latter acted across the three-dimensional surface to produce gravitation.

How may we quantitatively check all the above's apparent complexity? By taking our cue from the first principles of surface tension. It was found by C. Vernon Boyes that the pressure inside a soap bubble always varies inversely as its radius, and he originated a very striking demonstration; so striking that any acquisitive reader might make a little cash by inducing a greenhorn to bet on the outcome. He arranged two separate soap bubbles, A and B, as shown in Figure 1, with interconnecting tubes and a three-way tap.

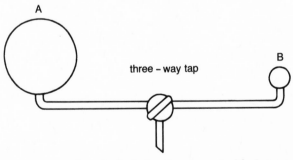

Figure 1. Demonstrating the Relative Pressures inside Interconnected Soap-bubbles

When the tap is turned to connect A and B, to everyone's surprise A bulges and B collapses. The excess pressure inside a soap bubble may be shown to be equal to $4Tr^{-1}$, where T is the surface tension acting along both sides of the surface, r being the radius of the bubble (cm). More relevant to gravitation, the excess pressure inside a spherical drop, equals $2Tr^{-1}$, where r is the the radius (cm) of the only surface to consider. But because the force of gravity has always been defined conventionally as that between two one-gram masses one centimeter apart, we should divide it by two when comparing it with a single mass, respecting surface tension. Thus the gravitational constant at the beginning of time, G, say when r was small (1.51 Å), may be equated with the present constant G, say by the simple equation:

$$(1), \qquad G_p = G_o\, r_p^{-1},$$

where G_p is the present gravitational constant, G_o, the gravitational constant at the beginning of time, and r_p the present radius of the Universe in Å units. We should think that at some critical moment in the past, the force of gravity, which once held electricity in check, at last gave way. At this point of exact balance, e may be equated with G_o as follows:

$$(2), \qquad e^2 = M^2\, G_o,$$

where e is the charge on an electron, and M the mass of an H atom(cm). The rationale underlying equations (1) and (2) is very important, because it shows the exact way in which electric force once operated to generate the observed intensity of the deep past. At the beginning of time, we should think that the universe lay like a seed or an egg, restricted only by an extreme gravitation. Then came the advent of the electric explosion. At this critical moment the radius of the universe was only 1.51 × Å,* i.e., the size of a hydrogen atom. Today, owing to expansion at the velocity of light, the universal radius has become:

2 × 10^{10} years (Hubble's constant) C cm/sec.
= 2 × 10^{10} × 31,500,000 × C cm.

*The Handbook of Chemistry and Physics (Cleveland, Ohio: Chemical Rubber Publishing Co., 1981).

51

$$= 2 \times 10^{10} \times 3.15 \times 10^7 \times 3 \times 10^{10} \text{ cm}$$
$$= 2 \times 10^{10} \times 3.15 \times 10^7 \times 3 \times 10^8 \text{Å, or } 1.92 \times 10^{36} \text{Å};$$
so that the expansion has occured 1.25×10^{36} times, or
$r_p = 1.25 \times 10^{36} \, r_o$, but:
$G_o = G_p \, r_p$, where G_o and G_p are the respective gravitational constants at zero time and at the present, as per equation(1).

Equation(2) arises from the definitions of gravity and electricity, as forces emanating from two sources, each obeying the law of inverse squares. Thus,

$$\frac{G_o = e^2 \, r^2 \text{ (electric force)}}{G_p = M^2 \, r \, G_p \text{ (gravitational force)}}$$

The above equation simplifies by cancelling, equal terms from denominator and numerator to:
$G_o = e^2 M^{-2}$, a form of equation(2). Combining equations (1) and (2), we get:
$G_p = e^2 M^{-2} \, r^{-1}$, dyne, $gm^{-2} \, cm^{-2}$.
Filling in recognised values: $G_p = (4.8)^2(10^{-20})(1.66)^{-2}(10^{-48})^2 =$ a final value of: 6.8×10^{-8}, dn, gm^{-2}. cm^{-2}. This estimate has been derived only from firmly established physical constants—e and M are known with great accuracy; so that our calculation comes quite close to the empirically observed and internationally recognised value of 6.67×10 dyne, cm^{-2}, gm^{-2}. We should, therefore, regard the calculation as buttressing the general idea of dead-beat time, and the reigning of intense gravity in the deep past. In fact, it constitutes certain verification.

Thus we see how many of the extraordinary observations of modern astronomy, high densities and orbital velocities, can be easily and simply reconciled with established science. There is no need to imagine black holes, white holes, worm holes, or even hyperboles. There is a possibility that optical images of distant satellites may at one time have been so warped by the intense gravity of early days that synchronous views of the same object could appear from either sides of a massive star.

There is now the appearance of a pervasive unification and economy. Science seems to be all of one piece. Longstanding puzzles, like the origin of the solar system, Olber's paradox, and the spiraling and oblation of galaxies can be cleared up. A new aspect of the structures of the chemical elements might be suggested. Instead of 2, 8, 18, 18 electron shell systems, we see that there may be but one. The octet could be recognised as a double tetrahedron; thus focussing on carbon as the apotheosis of the elements. Its nearest rival, the hydrogen molecule, H_2, could form a pseudo tetrahedron based on resonance. The priority for the future should now be the proper interpretation of electric force and the enormous electric energy potential of the atom as per Chapter 6.

To summarise, we may be driven to think that the so-called objective world is really quite ephemeral and temporal, a passing phase. The solid and lasting universe may be foursquare, stretchng out to encompass our four-dimentional selves and existing for ever in a setting that is more or less comfortable according to our life works.

Chapter 6

The Nature of Cooling

In Science, the simplest explanation carries conviction in proportion to its simplicity.

—Sir James Jeans

In Chapter 5 we saw, in exact terms, how gravitation was incidental to electricity and was no more a fundamental force than friction, adhesion, or tension. Gravity arose from the myriad dipoles of the physical world and we saw how it was a variable factor, dependent inversely on the radius of a visible yet finite universe. How may we be quite certain that electricity is, in fact, gravitation's progenitor? Simply because we all accept that electromagnetic radiation has a constant velocity, which is C. It signifies its consistency and control by flashing its signature with the lines of the Balmer and Lyman series. These appeared, even at the first moment of creation some 2×10^{10} years ago with the big bang.

Now we have to return to the fundamental nature of cooling because it may help us to unravel the fine structure of the electron itself. In Chapter 1, we described how Newton's cooling really established the basis for thermodynamics, which itself sprang from Newton's original dynamics. Its curves may have been broadly exponential, but they were also akin to their prototype at absolute zero temperature—the hyperbola. The gas equation is a combination of Boyle's law: (i), $PV = K$ being a constant; with: (ii), $TV = K$, Charles's or Gay-Lussac's Law, where T and V are temperature and volume variables at constant pressure, and K, another constant. The gas equation thus becomes: (iii), $PV = RT$, where R is the gas constant. Because R is a constant, the variable T must include both

P and V, so that the variation of T leads to a hyperbola within a hyperbola. In fact, the gas equation underlies the quantum theory. Radiation is a form of heat; and this electron, generated and particulate motion is a form of kinetic energy.

The quantum equation, $E\lambda = h$, where E is energy, and λ the wavelength, h being Planck's constant of action, shows that all types of heat are dynamic, i.e., kinetic.

When we consider that Newton described gravity a hundred years before Cavendish determined its solar constant, and when we remember that Cavendish was, all that much later, still a fervent believer in "phlogiston," we begin to glimpse Newtonian prescience. Shallow minds have reviled his waste of time on alchemy. But it was only the depth of his practical experience with furnaces and their varying intensities, which led him to formulate the first generalisation about heat loss, embracing all aspects of heat energy. How may we begin to appreciate the peculiarly unpredictable characteristics of cooling? There is a very elementary, yet illustrative, experiment using a large beaker of water heated by a Bunsen burner. First take a clean beaker and half-fill it with clean tap water. As the temperature rises, it becomes apparent that minute bubbles are beginning to form randomly in the water. This experiment used to be carried out with some trepidation; not only because of a tendency to "bumping" (superheating) but also because of the poor thermal qualities of the then standard glass. I was at school when World War I broke out, and the British laboratory glassware of those days was notably inferior to the Jena glass previously supplied. The Germans then specialised in chemistry in a rather similar way to present day concentration of the Japanese on silicon chips. German chemical industry thrived largely owing to its better understanding of steriochemical theory. After Bismark, chemistry had become an important part of general education. These developments helped Germany enormously during the war, in the supply of both high-explosives and poison gas. On the other hand, French chemistry became bogged down with its insistence on the arithmetrical aspect of organic chemistry, thus their dye industry faded.

To continue with the water-heating experiment using im-

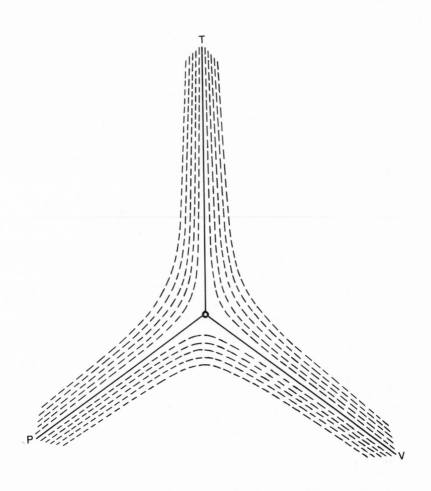

Figure 1. Hyperbolae Generated by the Gas Equation

proved glass-ware, the randomness of the bubbles is an indication of disordered energy throughout the water. But if this is too pure, or if it contains traces of amino acids, there arises the danger of superheating. In some way complexes of water molecules aggregate together to form positive indications of order. This amounts to an indication that hydrogen, with only one electron per atom, may somehow join other atoms together, and so split their affinity. In fact water is accepted as a typical associating solvent, and its complexes are thus able to disperse polar molecules, e.g., common salt. The ordered complexes of water may themselves be further dispersed, using "bumping stones" made from pieces of porous pottery ware. If the heating of boiling water is gradually discontinued, the bubbles slowly diminish in diameter, and ultimately disappear again in a random fashion. This illustrates the randomness of cooling. We shall see later how hydrogen bonding may be able to account for life with all its multiple processes. To properly understand cooling, we have to think carefully how kinetic energy might disappear. We know that water is molecular, and that when it evaporates away, it finally leaves as single, individual molecules. The process ends abruptly when the last one goes. Accurate observations near absolute zero temperature show that kinetic energy drains in a similar way so that we ought to think of kinetic energy as existing in minute, discrete bundles. We may well imagine an atom of energy as a kind of minute sphere, a moving microhypersphere. This is a long three-syllable word, which might, for short be called "micre." A micre could move either by transference or spin. It might be similar in many ways to water, H_2O. Triatomic water might be the prototype for triatomic energy. Mass is dominant over space and time, just as oxygen is central to its attendant hydrogens. Thus a micre could approximate to what is now known as a neutrino.

We have already seen how a massive influx of neutrinos could account for the pressure behind the dead-beat wave of time, and how this pressure could account quantitatively for gravitation and the remarkably intense gravitation and fields of energy observed using optical and longer E/M-wave telescopes (see Chapters 3 and 5). A micre could move by transfer or spin, but in order to account quantitatively for its energy, it should move at the limiting velocity of light. Thus, a single electromagnetic impulse, a photon, might signify a single revolution at peripheral velocity C. An eddying micre might be lapping in a ring at velocity C to signify an electron. This requires a definite axis which might, for economy, be taken over by the third fundamental—mass—the axis of being.

The test of any theory is practical. How then does the spinning micre agree with what we already know about electrons? What about their energy, their mass, and attraction (e) for their opposite charge (also e)? An electron has one unknown quality—its radius, say r. The outward centrifugal force inside a spinning ring* is known to be mv^2r^{-1} where m is its mass, v its velocity and r its radius of spin. The electronic charge e exerts $4.8^2 \times 10^{-20}$ dynes when two such charges are exactly 1 cm apart. If they are r cm apart the force becomes e^2r^{-2} dynes. We can now form an equation:

$$mv^2r^{-1} = e^2r^{-2}$$
so that (iii), $r = e^2m^{-1}v^{-2}$ cm

If v for an electron is its natural, ultimate speed in space/time, C, r becomes 2.82×10^{-13} cm. The ultimate unit of length is 5.64×10^{-13} cm. or 5.64×10^{-5} Å. This might also be the approximate diameter of all 92 atomic nuclei.

Having evaluated r the approximate radius of an electron, we can now find its energy, which is simply, e^2r^{-1} ergs : 8.2×10^{-7} ergs. To convert ergs to grams, we apply the mass/energy relation. and divide by C^2 (9×10^{20}) giving 9.1×10^{-28} g (internationally accepted value from cathode ray analysis : $9.1066 \pm 0.0032 \times 10^{-28}$ g). The interaction of X-rays of the shortest wavelength about 10^{-9} cm, with atoms (Compton effect), shows that the quantum of energy associated with this radiation is also sufficient to allow the formation of an electron and account for its mass: again 9.1×10^{-28} g. Thus we have a relation (equation iii) which brings together mass/energy, quantum theory, and centrifugal force, giving a further accurate verification of our hypothesis.

The ratio of electronic charge to mass was first evaluated by J. J. Thompson's cathode ray analysis. But the ratio of charge to

*In a direction opposite to the course of the sun (counterclockwise).

radius of spin is especially interesting, because it may give us a clear insight into the mode of the creation of an electron. We mostly concur that there should be some kind of initial backcloth to existence. And we might think that before the big bang that background could have been an almost infinite expanse of inert and static micres. Then came a gentle influx of rotary energy inducing spin. Here Newton's third law may have come into play. Every forward turn invoked a "widdershins" reverse turn. The spin of one micre induced attraction on the surface of neighbouring micres. This also originated a short-range cohesion, Coulomb forces, and the law of inverse squares.

Let us try to imagine the original creation process. First we should visualise a wide expanse of inert micres, each hollow but minutely hyperspherical, a vast shell beach, rather like the one at Herm near Guernsey. A single hypersphere is like a sphere, but with an extra fundamental dimension. Spheres themselves may be seen as multiframeworks of great circles, crossing each other at all angles. They are geodesic, similar to the infrastructure of the wings and frame of the RAF Wellington bombers during the war. Thus the prototype of both a sphere and a hyersphere is a simple circular ring. To visualise spin, we should see it as beginning with a ring spinning about its central transverse axis. The movement essentially follows Newton's second law. Thus the uniform acceleration would be seen to continue to the limits of spin. Just as a particle might accelerate uniformly along a line to its limiting speed C, so a ring too, should ultimately reach its limiting peripheral velocity. Cm : mass $\times r$: radius, as per mass/energy, mC^2.

Having seen how an electron might have come into being, we can now imagine the creation of its opposite, a proton. Centrifugal force always acts outwardly, and when a spinning micre reaches its limit of spin and radius, it forms an electron—a negatron. What, exactly, may have happened to its opposite and reverse creation? First we should think that the induced force acts in reverse. The spinning electron faced forward along the axis of time and directly followed its arrowhead so that the reverse process should be backwards into the past. The induced reaction should thus become inner and centripetal not outward. It is fundamentally different. Instead of reaching an equilibrium it continued to drive micres to the centre, as opposed to the circumference. In this way it induced a reverse attraction. Micres were piled up, not in space, nor yet in time, but into being, along the "unseen" dimension of mass. It is all quite similar to the reaction of air molecules in a jet aero engine. The plane, as a whole, moves forward, but the intensely compressed exhaust gases shoot even more rapidly backwards (often producing a telltale trail of condensed water vapour droplets from burnt hydrocarbons). Thus we see how a negative congenitor, a negatron, may have induced a positive reaction, a proton, the two particles being generated in close proximity. Thereafter they mutually attracted each other to form neutrons long before the big bang. Neutrons are dipoles known to induce gravitation (see Chapter 5). They could thus set up a subsequent, originating explosion—the big bang. In this way the explosion ensured the generation of all the known chemical atoms of the physical world. Streams of dynamic micres, neutrinos, attracted by nuclei, would then set up a self-perpetuating system and incidentally supply the pressure needed to keep up the passage of time (see Chapter 5).

Why do we feel certain that this is the correct and authentic history of the universe? First, because our estimate of the ultimate unit of space—5.6×10^{-13} cm forms not only the link between gravity, electricity, and mass/energy, but it is also surprisingly close to Rutherford's estimate (1911) based on the scattering of alpha particles.* Here we have to remember that alpha particles approaching other heavy positive nuclei must be subject to a strong repulsion, because the alpha particles themselves might also form centres for incoming micres. It is a case of like charges avoiding one another, and so making the passage of an alpha particle surprisingly easy, and, incidentally, head-on collisions surprisingly rare.

The abovequoted figure reminds us of Rutherford's dictum: "We can take the radius of an atomic nucleus to be about one ten

---

*According to *The Handbook of Chemistry and Physics* (Cleveland, Ohio: Chemical Rubber Co., 1947), p. 2627, the mean radius from viscosity, Van der Waals equation and heat conductivity methods, is given as $1.5\text{Å} = 1.5 \times 10^{-8}$ cm; for the monatomic atoms of helium, argon, krypton, and xenon. Rutherford's one ten thousandth part of the above figure, would give 1.5×10^{-12} cm, to compare with our calculated value of 0.56×10^{-12} cm.

thousandth part of that of an atom." It also reminds us of Newton's description of atoms as being "so very hard, as never to wear out or break in pieces." The revelation that atoms were mostly empty was not at all in accord with, or to the liking of, the then accepted opinion, and Professor Perkin disputed it. Innovators are often treated with disbelief or even derision. Copernicus was an upstart, Newlands was advised to try classifying the Chemical elements by their initial letters! Marconi could not expect to send electromagnetic radiation between the continents because of the natural curvature of the Earth! Nor could Acheson expect any chemical combination between carbon and silicon, because both these elements were next to one another in the same periodic group! More recently, many jokes have been made about both Eddington and Dirac concerning their so-called dimensionless numbers. Rutherford replied to Perkin that it was difficult to think of anything quite like a nucleus. Then he reflected: "Now I have it. It is something small; and hard and round, and very, very dense; in fact; well-nigh impenetrable; quite like Professor Perkin's head!" Judging by the way the hypersphere has been received over the last thirty years, well-nigh impenetrable heads are very common.

Chapter 7

The Escape through Becoming

The world was all before them, where to choose
Their place of rest . . .
— Milton, *Paradise Lost*

At all times throughout history people have attempted to escape from themselves—from the world, from the "City of Destruction," from "the body of this death." But hitherto feelings of frustration have not been quite so acute, because only in the present age have the hard confines of the world seemed so accurately and inexorably defined. Hitherto it has always seemed possible to imagine ill-defined regions or states where the inescapable drudgeries and basics of life might be simplified or are non-existent. The picture now recognised and accepted as real is one bounded by space and time; and since Descartes, these limits have been increasingly considered in mathematical terms. This fundamental trend ought to be carefully checked. And although it may seem more idiotic and pretentious than tilting at windmills to challenge the assembled nexus of mathematical thought, yet insight only arises from criticism. In recent years it is mathematics that has aggressively invaded the thinking of the ordinary man, and disastrously coloured the whole collective mind. From its cooperative but auxiliary place beside natural philosophy, it has suddenly emerged to take control with mimimal dissent, largely because of the acknowledged intricacies and technicalities of the subject. People, in general, are diffident about even simple math, so that many intelligent pundits have found it expedient to join the mathematical bandwagon and airily observe that "There are now no ultimates nor absolutes," or "The passage of time is a myth."

Why should so abstruse a theory have so wide and far-reaching an influence? It is because there is always, in every age, an intense contention to find the clearest, hardest, and intellectually crowning picture of reality, the sharpest, most consistent, and most economical pattern of collective thought? This then becomes the vogue picture, and it effectively reigns in society, pervading and infiltrating every layer, colouring, and conditioning its entire consciousness.

Thus in the clear skies of ancient Egypt, the reigning pattern was astronomical. Were not the stars in their courses the most reliable and permanent guides amid an otherwise painfully random, disorganised, and destructive world? This pattern was not only mentally comforting, but it yielded dividends—it allowed the prediction of the annual inundation, which in turn enabled sufficient corn to be sown and reaped to support an army of slaves.

The slaves in turn developed their own even more economical pattern. There was only one, not many, supernatural influences in the sky—a father who might lead his children from slavery to a promised land. This pattern was taken up and expanded by Christianity so that, apart from allowing an escape from slavery, the whole idea eventually became abhorrent and an anathema, intolerable to all civilised men. The rise of Christianity and its merging with Greek philosophy then formed the basis for the three-tier universe; and this became the successor theme.

With the Renaissance and the Rise of Science, the reigning picture was greatly broadened and expanded. The sun, not the Earth, was at the centre of the universe. This continued until all activities, forces, and influences were explained as changes in a universal, background ocean, the luminiferous ether; and this became the effective inheritor.

It is at this point that mathematics began to take over. It may seem surprising that so hedging and circumspect a discipline should even aspire or dare to provide a picture. But we must remember that mathematics is a language, and that words are symbols that originated from mosaics of elementary pictures. In fact the power of the human mind to create its own original pictures is its greatest attribute. The valuable contribution of mathematics centres on economy, yet its merit is not the elimination of ultimates but of extravagance in their use. Economy is important because the pruning out of any unnecessary assumptions increases credibility. But we delude ourselves if we think that mathematics has no need of ultimates. For example, it makes the assumption of identical units, both positive and negative, and of zero and infinity. In the development of analysis it presupposes that space and time are transverse to one another. Yet in its zeal for economy, it ran into oversimplification. The scalpel was applied with too heavy a hand; something was swept away which ought to have been left. One such tempting but unjustified parsimony was the idea that time is just a temporal order, a historical series, a "pattern of timeless moments."

Just now we mentioned the scapel, but a closer analogy might have been the filleter's knife. In the old days, if you went to a fishmonger to buy a plaice or a sole, he would ask: "Do you want it filleted?" Filleting was a marvelous operation that enabled the customer to taste all the flavour of fish without running the risk of swallowing a fishbone. But the fishmonger still popped the question, because there were a few people who averred to prefer their fish on the bone. Thus mathematicians have found it expedient to fillet time, and simply treat a unit of it as though it were a pound of lard or any other commodity. It made mechanics easy; but it was best to say as little as possible about the operation, because essentially time had been filleted, mutilated, and reduced to a flabby caricature.

If something is slightly incongruent at one point, it is likely to be so at other points. Thus the Procrustean and jaundiced approach of mathematics in its appraisal of the physical world shows discrepancies in several directions. In biology for example, the central and coordinating theme is evolution, which, since its inception, has deepened and broadened in scope almost without limit. There was once supposed to be a yawning gap between the then simplest forms of biological life—the amoeba and the inorganic and physical world. But research and developments in biochemistry have demonstrated that the imagined gap does not exist. There appears to be the probability of evolution from atoms, through more and more complex molecules, to the recognisably simplest units of life, and the time-scale gap available is quite as long as that taken by single cells themselves to reach the more complex and coordinated multicellular types current today. It has become clear that evolution should include, not merely the development of biological species, but the whole gamut of changes that have occurred during observed astronomical time. Thus the order and complexity found even in elementary atoms and their interreactions to form innumerable micro and macro molecular combinations, as well as the evolving forms of stars and galaxies, can all be fitted into one trend.

The mathematician is asking us to accept that the above process amounts to a predetermined unfolding of inevitable events. From a primeval cloud of hydrogen everything else is supposed to arise automatically. On this basis the emergence of water might have been expected by extrapolation from its congeners in the same periodic group to have produced a gas even lighter than hydrogen sulphide, whereas in fact, the emergent hydride turned out to have the very unpredictable and exceptional qualities that permitted the further emergence of biological species.

During the last century there has been a preeminent effort to investigate and understand the ultimate particles of matter. Here again, although the concept of time as a mere scale was taken to be fundamental, yet the attack was somewhat frustrated, because when more became known about the atomic world, its future along time became more unpredictable. All that could be positively inferred was that the unpredictability in the past had risen and fallen rhythmically, taking the form of a wave. The emergence of a wave form should have indicated that time itself was unlikely to be just a linear series, because it is axiomatic that waves always arise from the interplay of two transverse variables.

Another preeminent concern of physics has been the development of thermodynamics, a science very much involved with the direction of time. Straightaway the arrow indicator demanded by the second law favours a flow hypothesis. But mathematicians may argue that the direction only shows a herringbone pattern pointing in the direction of time. Against this we have to weigh the observed downfall of parity in the production of elementary particles in nuclear processes. These are dynamic changes also backed by the biochemical observation that dextrorotatory isomers are more numerous in nature than the laevo ones, and were time a symmetrical axis, exactly equal concentrations of the two isomers might have been expected.

Curiously enough it is in the science of mechanics itself that the inadequacy of the dead-scale view is most vividly exposed. If time is something more than a dead-scale, what extra dimension or dimensions should be added to make it credible and provide a fresh picture of existence? There have been many suggestions concerning a further sort of time: time embracing time, eternal time, eternity, et cetera, but always there has been the great objection that another time leads on to an infinite and vicious regression of times, as in J. W. Dunne's serialism.

First we ought carefully to consider a simple duality. Mechanics teaches that there are two and only two prototypes of motion: straight progression and rotation. All movement, e.g., wave-motion, is resolvable into these two types; they produce analogous equations of motion and related qualities. Thus angular velocity-acceleration-momentum, moment of inertia and torque correspond closely with linear velocity-acceleration-momentum, mass, and force. Both linear and angular momenta are conserved, and there are parallel sets of equations. Similarly there are only two kinds of change—steady and accelerated. Acceleration generates angular velocity by a proportional increase in pitch. These dual prototypes demonstrate that time comprises two parameters: you can only properly symbolise acceleration by presupposing a third (Z) axis, becoming perpendicular to the time (X) and space (Y) axes of a space/time diagram. The whole of extension is now filled.

It is often forgotten that we have no reliable way of measuring time. Clocks are contrivances designed to move at a steady speed, linear or angular, so that when we think we are measuring time, we are comparing velocities by measuring the proportionate space or angle covered by the clock. The terms *minutes* and *seconds* arose in this way: they were originally minutes and seconds of *arc*. Thus when we construct a space/time diagram, a programme or a time-table, we are simply comparing space against space; the actual time remains as elusive as ever. Here mathematicians argue in a circle. They first suppose time to be space, and then by a long algebraic deduction finally discover that time *is* space and takes parity to form a four-dimensional continuum. To really compare space against time, we need three axes: one to represent space, one to represent the spatial factor of time (scale-time), and one to represent time itself (becoming). The extensiveness of existence is now complete.

Velocity and acceleration are also linked together in another intriguing way, which clearly demonstrates that they signify two quite separate and dimensional aspects of passing time. The former induces magnetism when electric charges move, while the latter produces gravity-linked inertia when material particles change their speeds. Were velocity and acceleration merely the first and second differentials, respectively, of space against dead-scale time, as in the series $\dot{x}, \ddot{x}, \dddot{x}, \ldots$, then a rate of change of acceleration ought to produce some quite special and unique physical effect and quality, which, so far, no one has either observed or produced. We have all experienced the thrill of seeing a falling star against the dark night sky. Its fall certainly generates heat, light, and perhaps sound, but although it undergoes a steady increase in acceleration along with its ever-closer approach to an ever-intensifying gravitational field, no special unexplained physical effect is produced; whereas the two unique kinds of change, velocity and acceleration, are underwritten and guaranteed by magnetism and inertia, two great pillars of physics.

Considering again the series $\dot{x}, \ddot{x}, \dddot{x}, \ldots$, we have to ask ourselves actually to relate these differential processes to the physical world, rather than to slavishly follow the rules of analysis, which are like the grammatical rules of a language—physicists stick to mathematics as the schoolmen stuck to Latin. Before the Rosetta stone was discovered, Egyptologists had already accumulated sufficient hieroglyphical sequences to establish a language of some sort. It was soon found that a crude grammar could be discerned, showing the connection between the symbols, although actual meanings remained obscure. Thus the possibility arose of inventing or imagining symbols that could follow the rules, yet which did not correspond with actual objects current in ancient Egypt. A similar circumstance has arisen in the language of mathematics. With the development of the calculus, it soon became clear that an expression that could be differentiated could, in some cases, be integrated. Furthermore each differentiation or integration signified the loss or gain of a dimension. The first differential of a line becomes a point, which still denotes the slope of that line; while the integration of the line gives an area, the area under the curve. In mechanics, velocity is the slope, while the area is proportional to the kinetic energy or work done on a moving object. The Irishman W. R. Hamilton (1805–1865) established these ideas in the first half of the nineteenth century, and he therefore logically inferred that there must be an infinite number of imaginary dimensions to take care of an infinitude of possible differentiations and integrations. In particular, whereas people generally were well aware of the three spacial dimensions, Hamilton could imagine a fourfold space, and its functions became known as quaternions. The subject grew into vector analysis, which is the basis for modern mathematical physics.

Where mathematics lost its anchor was in keeping to rules rather than to insight. We should all know that the physical world is bounded by the three dimensions of space: north/south, east/west, up and down. Existence is also bounded by three dimensions: space, time, and becoming. We all know instinctively that it is right and natural to set these dimensions transversely to one another. When we come to the first differential against time, we have a set ratio of space to time, ds/dt, at a point, which foreshadows a straight line, a relation showing an extra dimension: similarly with the second differentiation. Only a parabola, $s = \frac{1}{2} at^2$, can produce a straight line by differentiation, and the parabola encloses an area within its curve indicating the appearance of two dimensions. Conversely, if the first integration of a line gives an area, the second integration must give a volume. But here the reality ends because we have run out of real dimensions; a real three-dimensional solid effectively scotches the vicious regress started by Hamilton's infinite dimensions. Just as the area under a curve symbolises the reality of the work or energy involved, so the volume swept out by a curve is a token of the real creation taking place. Here we have a rationale for the expanding universe—the natural acceleration brought about by the exercise of gravity and its continuous output of newly created volume may balance continuous discreation at black holes.

It is especially interesting that analysts naturally underrate acceleration, because they instinctively take their subject as beginning and being confined to a plane of space and time; acceleration goes outside that plane. They are at pains to point out that Newton's second law does not even mention acceleration, and describes force as rate of change of momentum, quite forgetting that Newton, in his *Principia*, built his science of dynamics around rate of change of velocity, for which he designated the symbol f to represent the Latin *feste*, which means quickening or bringing to life and creation, as in festivity.

Philosophy has also greatly underrated Newton's second law: $p = mf$ (p, force, m, mass). Yet the importance of feste can hardly be exaggerated. Whereas prosaic matter has been glorified and elevated into the basis for a great system, materialism, the other more lively and significant factor, feste, has been quite neglected. It stands for something much more than bare ideas; it includes the will to carry them out and bring them to creation and reality. Changes in any material system can only be brought about as the resultant of applied force or forces; and the application of force only arises from a change of mind and will. When a runner sprints to win the mile, or a batsman presses to top the opposing score, or a driver decides to get somewhere in a shorter time, they all use their respective festes to mould the future. Thus feste implies a simultaneous change in both space and scale-time, and therefore its expression demands its own transcendent dimension. Because the entire universe is changed and actuated by force, and force is enlivened by feste, this must signify the very ground and depth of all existence and being. We have seen that feste is an expression of will and creativity so that it is clear that the universe is personal, and that every minutest part has its own individual contribution, its own modicum of free will. Newton was a deeply religious man and, theologically, his unitarianism was years ahead of his time. Had he progressed a little more into dynamics, he might have given the world a third great commandment: "Thou shalt direct thy feste towards the creation of a better world."

We know only two certain things about this paramount dimension of becoming: its parity of unfoldment with, and its transverse direction to, scale-time; everything else is mystery and conjecture. This is as it should be. A true and satisfactory picture should be open-ended. It should give a perspective that fades into a dim horizon, leaving a feeling of awe and wild surmise. The realisation of becoming is like climbing Slieve League in Donegal. From the northeast it looks like another fairly symmetrical mountain or steep windswept hill, such as you might find anywhere in central Wales or Scotland. Then at the top, surprise of surprises, the mountain seems sliced by a knife and drops sheerly into the Atlantic nearly two thousand feet below. A faint murmur of the sea blends into the rugged coastline stretching far into Sligo and beyond. Looking back at flat space and time from the vantage of becoming, the inadequacy of the conventional mathematical picture is more apparent. It totally ignores becoming and vainly endeavours to seal up the majesty and wonder of nature into a neat and tidy package.

All that mathematics can positively suggest is that your framework of reference, your self-centredness, your point of view is as valid as anyone else's; and this principle has increasingly flourished since the advent of the twentieth century. As we said at the beginning, the vogue picture pervades every walk of life, and its principles filter far and wide. Today's vogue is mathematical, and though its authors are well-intentioned, they cannot prevent the spread and consequences of their ideas. The nation states, in particular, have pursued their own self-centred interests, resulting in the growth of strife and war. The clash of evil has produced yet more evil, so that today humanity teeters on the brink of collapse. All that we hold dear: kindness, grace, patience, humility, heroism, et cetera, are in retreat.

What mathematics is doing by taking existence to be simply bounded by space and scale-time, is to cut the real world into two, discarding present and future, and considering only the dead recorded past. By this act it cuts itself off from the living mainstream of humanity, which has accepted the passage of time as the very foundation and essence of being. How then can the findings and principles of mathematics be fitted into a fuller, more complete and universal picture? It is as though a complex of space and temporal extension provide a backcloth on which the picture of existence is projected. It is this process of projection that brings the backcloth to life; and it is the process of becoming that supplies the quality we know as life. This screen-based dynamic projection reminds us of the old defunct three-tier universe—it saw the world as a stage set between pit and gods. Both have the merit of presenting a definite image that any or everyone may embrace and continue to keep in sharp focus. When it comes to a comparable simple mathematical picture, we are in a quandary. It is clear that time is part of the real world, yet mathematics accepts only three axes for real space, so that scale-time has to be modified in some way; and this is done by defining time as an imaginary dimension with the inclusion of the square-root of minus one. Unfortunately this factor is infinitely abstract, and though the picture may be satisfactory to mathematicians, its general acceptance is restricted.

More particularly our screenlike projection sees the present as a wave proceeding at the velocity of light along the axis of scale-time. And this view embraces the development of vector-analysis and all the findings of relativity and quantum theories—the zone bounded by past scale-time and space is exactly that now considered by modern physics. The advancing wave not only explains the present, it fits in with the expanding universe and shows why opposed positive and negative charges do not cancel, and provides a rationale for the immense kinetic energy of atomic nuclei. The Fitzgerald-Lorentz contraction, over which relativity makes such heavy weather becomes a rider on Pythagoras.*

*The pithed mathematics of today fills no deep-felt hope for a reason: it just uses rules to compute figures. The simplest example of creation is seen in the swelling of a wave, and this can be reduced to two transverse motions: a general motion forward with velocity, v, giving a moiety of kinetic energy—$\frac{1}{2}mv^2$—and a cross-oscillation, peak velocity also, v, supplying the other moiety—$\frac{1}{2}mv^2$— giving mv^2 in all. If the waves are moving in a medium of fundamental wave velocity, C, their energy becomes mC^2. When the waves of matter, already moving through time with velocity C, are given a transverse velocity, v, the resultant waves produce the semblance of obliquity through time, still at speed C, because this is limiting for the medium. The resultant waves are slightly deflected, but their local time has changed its direction. This produces a right-angled triangle with the hypotenuse symbolised as C and the height as v. The base of the triangle becomes $\sqrt{C^2 - v^2}$, and a length inside the resultant wave appears reduced by the factor $1 - \sqrt{1 - (v^2/C^2)}$. Similarly the acquisition of transverse kinetic energy, $\frac{1}{2}mv^2$, increases the energy of the wave proportionately, and its mass increases to: $m/\sqrt{1 - (v^2/C^2)}$.

71

The backwards extrapolation of past scale-time points to an initial focal point coincident and consistent with the big bang origin of the universe. The curvature of its expanding hypersphere is quantitatively in agreement with a past scale-time of about 2×10^{10} years, a figure strikingly confirmed by the echo of the initial explosion arriving from all points of space. This figure of 2×10^{10} years is also consistent with a gravitational constant of 6.65×10^{-8} dyne $cm^2 g^{-2}$, if we take gravity to be inversely proportional to radius of curvature. Thus we see how a new universal and comprehensive vision emerges, which is consistent with the findings of science, yet at the same time embraces all the long recognised principles of ideal conduct and behaviour.

Chapter 8

The Riddle of the Molecule

I am at work on the humming loom of time.
And so produce the Godhead's living garment.
—Goethe

It has long been realised that the ultimate and underlying fine structure of the physical world is electrical. The electromagnetic theory of radiation also harmonises smoothly with this concept of atoms as centres of attraction and repulsion. It is therefore unfortunate that orthodox quantum and relativity physics seem unable to penetrate the central and essential mystery of electric force. Further, electrical attractions and repulsions signify wave motion, rhythm, and tempo. Perhaps the difficulty stems from the relapse of mechanics into a static concept. Mechanics since Newton has given up its dynamism and has steadfastly refused to inquire into the nature and origin of force. Thus vector analysis began with the difficult concept of "least action." Action itself has been defined as the product of work by time. But work itself has already been defined as the product of force by distance equivalent to kinetic energy. The multiplication by time only serves to eliminate acceleration. In so doing it destroys the essential feature of Newton's second law. Static forces have lost their tempo, and cannot be compared with dynamic forces. A pair of equal and opposite forces are supposed to cancel each other, yet they are still able to be resolved into components at right angles. Forces are described as vectors, which are claimed to be utterly and absolutely revealed as straight lines in one plane. The word *acceleration* itself is derived from *feste*, to hasten, thus implying thought and decision. Thus the tempo of time cannot change without an act of will.

Physical theory ought to help in the unravelling of chemical bonding. In handbooks of chemistry and physics there are sections describing estimated sizes of atoms, where values derived from wave-mechanics jostle uncomfortably with other values derived from classical considerations; the lack of correlation is glaring. Now compare this disarray with the climate seventy years ago. Then every schoolboy learned by heart that atomic volume = atomic weight/density; and every honours candidate could expect a leading question on the subject. Were not the cyclical swings of the atomic volume curve first demonstrated by Lothar Meyer in 1870, a main pillar of the periodic law? And had not Professor Soddy found that lead from his radioactive transitional series possessed exactly the same atomic volume as ordinary lead, showing that the index was even more fundamental than either of its two components? Today, the term *atomic volume* seems to have dropped out of the language. What is even more surprising is that this and other changes have come about without either dissent or discussion. Physical theory is appallingly threadbare about its own fundamentals. Not a word as to why positive and negative charges do not immediately fly together in mutual annihilation; no clue to explain how every atom manages to hold together such an enormous quota of energy, no rationale of Stefan's Law, nor of the Rayleigh four-power formula for radiation, and very little about atomic domains.

In Chapter 5 it was deduced that electric force was about 1.25×10^{36} times more potent than gravitational force: again the radius of the universe (2×10^{10} light years) compared with the radius of a neutral hydrogen atom (1.54×10^{-8} cm) came to the similar dimensionless number of 1.24×10^{36}. In Chapter 6, the existence of ultimate units of energy (quanta) was seen to lead naturally to an ultimate unit of space (2.84×10^{-13} cm), and further, to an ultimate unit of force by dividing the unit of energy (Planck's constant 6.62×10^{-27} erg) by the unit of space, the distance through which the force acted, giving a least value of 2.3×10^{-11} dynes. It is clear that the encapsulated space/time near a proton is likely to be limited by the rate the electric stress falls away to its lowest value (2.3×10^{-14} dynes). On the other hand the maximum stress between proton and electron should be $e^2 r^{-2} = 2.84 \times 10^6$ dynes,

74

so that the ratio between greatest and least stress becomes 1.20 × 10^{20} : 1. This ratio of negative electric forces acting near places of minimum and maximum stress close to a hydrogen nucleus can teach us something about conditions inside the four-dimensional space/time enclave we call a molecule. Superficially anyone might think that this tension near the nucleus ought to die away, as per Coulomb's law, in a similar way to electric, magnetic, heat, light, and sound effects, according to inverse squares. But there is something much more complex about the active spaces close to atomic nuclei. How might the nuclear tension decline with distance? First of all, we believe that an electron may never, even remotely, coincide with its positive counterpart. Their inverse peripheral rings may both be spinning oppositely at velocity C; and in this way set up a final, inexorable cosmic aversion.

In the introduction, we imagined the kinetic theory of gases, extending to cover not only gases and lone molecules, but also describing the lesser-sized electrons, to be found as basic particles, even in ordinary air. Assuming these electrons to be in thermodynamic equilibrium, we might view them as moving at an average speed of about one-thousandth of the speed of light, i.e., at ca. 160 miles per second. Here we have to remember that space/time near a nucleus is essentially four-dimensional, thus bringing it into harmony with Stefan's or Rayleigh's fourth-power relationship.

How does this four-dimensional picture of a molecule fit in with points of maximum and minimum electric stress, as per our calculations? We found a ratio of about 1.2 × 10^{20} : 1. Thus : $\sqrt{1.2 \times 10^{20}} = 1.04 \times 10^{5}$: 1. This factor has to be geared to r, (electron radius) 2.84 × 10^{-13} cm (see Chapter 6), giving slightly less than 3 angstrom units. This figure agrees reasonably closely with the observed values for hydrogen and other atoms. Thus: 1.04 × 10^{5} × 2.84 × 10^{-13} = 2.95 × 10^{-8} cm, or 2.95 Å. So far some quite hard values, the gravitational constant, the electron charge and mass, as well as atomic X-ray spacings and nuclear dimensions, have now been harmonised together into a single idea—the expanding hypersphere. This is what this book is all about. The ancients felt the same and were always looking for "the one in many." Socrates said he would follow the finder as a god. And indeed, his disciple, Aristotle, did introduce such a system, which lasted a thousand years. Shakespeare and his Great Globe arose from an Aristotelian context and preceded Newton. But in these latter days, culture has become divergent. New universities and their faculties, go ever more and more in their separate ways.

Having constructed a skeleton framework, we should continue by trying to fill it out. First, the molecule: a glimpse of gravitation as arising from dipoles leads to a lot more about the simple refraction of light by a transparent crystal. The dipoles in a crystal are very well-orientated and lined up. In sharp contrast, the incandescent matter of the sun is exceedingly random.

Refraction

If light from a distant star, grazing a limb of the sun, may be shown to suffer a slight deflection by the attraction of the sun's enormous gravity and its innumerable, if randomised dipoles, how much more may the refraction of light by a crystal give us a better idea of what really happens? According to the static concept of "least action," the velocity of light passing through a transparent body should be decreased. If this is really the case, how is it that the light finally emerging from the crystal should somehow have reacquired its original wavelength and constant velocity, C? We can only imagine that its light becomes somehow equally accelerated and then decelerated by its passage through the almost-perfect lattice of such a transparent solid. All the same, its path through the crystal must certainly have increased in length. In this way it must have suffered only an apparent loss of velocity. In effect, the light first accelerated, just as Newton said it would three hundred years ago. But later it must have suffered a reversing sequence of acceleration and deceleration, as it passed alternate positive and negative centres in the crystal. "Least action" seems to have got by superficially for 250 years. But the more anyone looks carefully into its proposals, the more improbable they seem. One colossal improbability arises from the fact that the wavelength of visible light varies between about seven thousand and four thousand A, whereas the radius of a photon, as well as that of both positive and negative electric charges are only of the order of 10^{-5} Å. This disproportion enormously reduces the possibility of a head-on collision. Experience with colloidal dispersions has demonstrated that photons never collide with even large colloidal particles. The photons are simply bent around them, as shown in the ultramicroscope. If such bending occurs with visible particles, how much more is it likely to occur when the charged electric centres are so much smaller and relatively more widely dispersed? Further, light waves are supposed to form a straight line, a direct path. And according to "least action," there should be an abrupt change when a photon strikes a solid object. Einstein's *Relativity* certainly showed the truth, when it demonstrated that space/time could be curved near the sun. The contortion inside a molecule must be even more intense. Even the twinkling of a star is known to be due to the bending of photons around air molecules.

Long ago it was noticed that red-hot iron changes its brightness with increased heat: White-hot was the highest temperature. These ideas were first expressed quantitatively as Wien's law:

(i), $T = W \lambda^{-1}$,

T being the temp, and λ the wavelength, with W, Wien's constant. Since the absolute temperature of a particle is directly proportional to its kinetic energy, equation (i) is equivalent to Planck's (ii), $E = hv$, v being the frequency and, h, Planck's constant.

Stefan's law arises when the number of degrees of electron freedom are multiplied fourfold as previously described. Hence:

(iii), $E = ST^4$,

E being the energy radiated per sec, on all wave-lengths, T the absolute temperature, and S Stefan's constant.

SIMPLE OPTICAL EFFECTS

These always originate from the repulsion set up between the like polarities of electrons and micre exteriors and it may be basically due to their like rotations. If an electron hole implies eddying, a quantum exterior could also be eddying in the same directive sense, and on approach, a repulsive force would naturally arise from the piling up of micres in between.

Reflection: This may be caused when an approaching negative photon is subsequently driven away at the speed of its approach. The surface of a metallic mirror is dense with negative electrons, while an oncoming quantum also shows a superficial negativity, hence repulsion. If, however, a photon sequence has a high frequency along its line of approach, e.g., X rays, the energy may be enough to allow penetration of the negative surface, and could even dislodge an electron (Compton effect).

Total Reflection: If a photon approaches a transparent solid of high refractive index (high negative surface potential), its angle of incidence from the normal may have to be small for it to penetrate, otherwise negative repulsion may completely prevent entrance and give total reflection. Photons show differences in negativity according to their frequency so that at any given moment, some with low polarity may penetrate, while others may have sufficient negativity to be reflected. There will, however, always be a critical angle from the normal, above which reflection will always occur. When a photon tries to exit from a solid it will again face the electronic surface barrier, so that once inside a solid of high polarity it may be partially trapped and have to undergo several internal reflections. Only when it achieves a suitably high angle of incidence may it succeed in escaping. Hence the brilliance of high index solids, e.g., diamond. The great merit of Newtonian dynamics was that it lived. It became an intimate and natural part of the magical elegance of motion. Here was something concerned with the real world and the continuous unfolding of existence. It led on to a dynamic and absolute view of time. This was in line with both the Greek and Christian roots of our Western civilisation: "Who will tell me that there are not three times, past, present, and future" and "Now, in the time of our mortal life, is the time." Whereas other religions are fatalistic, Christianity saw the "now" as salient from a dimmer, less important context. "The light of the world" was a spotlight charged with infinite possibilities. We feel this even as we passively watch television—live items are always more inter-esting than a record of things past. Dynamics may be declared dead, but once it played a vital part in the development of a com-plete and unified scientific nexus, ending with the quantum theory. At present this latter is translated into analytical terms, yet its ex-position offers no simple explanation of common electrical and optical phenomena.

The Alternative Dynamic Viewpoint

At the heart of dynamics is the clarification of motion as a transfer between matter, as a collection of atoms and void. Statics is able to imagine the extensiveness of space as lying transversely to that of time in a flat plane, thus producing a space/time diagram. This may be developed analytically, but it is still subject to the limitations of flatness. Though it may recognise changes in the slopes of its curves, it cannot countenance rotation about a third equivalent axis rising vertically from its plane. Therefore, it is un-able to throw any light on the most evident characteristic of that physical world, which it especially purports to describe: the reality of motion and change. Dynamics is more audacious. Even in Greek times, it could imagine the world (the universe) existing as a sea composed of particles of dense matter and void. Since matter could show a sharp edge, there must be a limit to its subdivision; there must be a stage beyond which it was impossible to cut it into some-thing smaller. These limiting units (atoms) were able to slip easily into the more extensive voids. The atomists Lucretius, Leucippus, Epicurus, and Democritus reacted to Elea by this scheme of atoms and voids. But the origins of atomism go even further into the past, and into the racial subconscious. Primitive man strove patiently and painfully, sometimes desperately, for the sharp edge, which should give him mastery over continuity. This tradition continues with the very symbol of time—an old man with a scythe.

It is a mistake to think that because atoms have now been transformed into an array of lesser particles, the atomic barrier no longer exists; that the sharp-edge argument is no longer valid. The overwhelming mass of the universe still exists as atomic nuclei, and the elusiveness and uncertainty about even the so well-explored electron remove it from any comparison with the solid proton. We shall see later that there are particles, also established by sharp-edge logic, which do form a sound and ultimate reference. The excitement of nuclear fission has paradoxically attracted many physicists away from the more prosaic, yet fundamental molecule. There is a great and far-reaching apostolic succession of atomism that defies being snuffed out like a candle by a hypothetical and partially undecipherable equation. Galileo, Gassendi, Mayow, Boyle, and Newton all passionately believed in atoms hundreds of years before Daltonian chemistry was even established as an exact science. Yet thenceforth it proceeded from strength to strength on that basis.

The Slippage into Void

Newton was able to imagine an even smoother way of slipping into void. The ancients conceded from practical experience that any proposed slippage would be attended by a natural resistance. Even air had to be moved out of the way if an arrow were to reach its target. But Newton saw that a moving body, removed far enough away from any interference by other matter, could slip into void with no resistance at all and as effortlessly as sunlight and shadow race across a field, hence his first law of motion. Just as statics rests on a comparison between the extensiveness of space and that of time, so the basis of dynamics depends on a comparison between the slipping of a moving body and the general slippage of time. In fact, all scientific discipline is based on strict and specific comparisons of like with like. In chemistry, atoms are compared with atoms. In physics, electric charges, heat, light, sound, densities, et cetera are compared with their respective units. In biology, species are compared with species. It is here that dynamics was thought to be wanting. The great criticism was that there was no discernable yardstick against which Newton's time might conceivably flow.

If we can check quantitatively the general and effortless slippage of the world (the universe) into void, then we have a yardstick.

More importantly we have a precise definition of the passage of time.* Just as Newton imagined how a moving object, isolated in space, might continue to slip without resistance, so can we also see the universe slipping without resistance. As we saw in Chapter 5, atoms could be waves in a universal sea of void; and the source of the atomic waves could be the original big bang. Thus we had an opportunity for that scientific verification so essential for the steady reinforcement of ideas. Newton saw the moon continuously falling to Earth at a steady speed; and he was able to calculate its observed acceleration from gravitational data on Earth. Similarly we say that gravity and electric dipoles were once in equilibrium (see Chapter 5); that the former's constant has uniformly declined from its original value, so that it is now only $10^{-36.33}$ of its former self, and that the world is continuously slipping into void at the speed of light.† In fact, gravity and the strong force which binds the atomic nucleus, turn out to be one and the same.

When it became possible actually to produce vacua and subject them to experiement, it became clear that empty space (void) was not entirely without properties. Electricity, light, magnetism, and gravitation were all carried at a steady, very fundamental speed—the velocity of light (C). It was found that light could cross the void without resistance, yet take time to do it by wave propagation, which a century ago required some sort of substratum, a backcloth or screen on which the panorama of existence might be enacted. The void seemed empty, but it could be energised to produce reality. So the "luminiferous ether" was invented. But the ether was a particularly spatial concept; and when the extensiveness of time was shown to match that of space, it ran into difficulties. Though analysts have developed field theories by deploying a number of imaginary dimensions and curvatures, they are still confronted by the great obstacle of explaining how A can influence B with nothing in between. On the other hand, the basic void of dynamics may comprise both the extensiveness of time and also that of space. Thus it may be expected to show those real characteristics that

*See Chapters 3 and 5.
†Hence its immense kinetic energy m C^2.

allow it to transmit forces, although the sources of the latter may originate from outside.

A hundred years ago dynamics was naturally applied to ultimate particles, especially those in the gaseous state. Here it became very fruitful as the kinetic theory, a generalisation that was used to explain many hitherto mysterious physical influences. It was applied to surface tension, viscosity, the specific heats of gases, elements and compounds, depressions of freezing points, elevations of boiling points, et cetera, culminating with thirteen independently derived, yet concordant values for Avogadro's number, 6.02×10^{23} molecules. Thus substances previously, but vaguely, described as being hot were clearly seen to owe their heat to the movement, translational or vibrational, of their molecules. This application of dynamics to heat gave us nineteenth century thermodynamics, along with three new basic laws to match those of the original mechanics. Application to electricity was also fruitful, giving a new discipline—electrodynamics, the concept of electrons as atoms of electricity followed. Above all electrodynamics clarified the nature both of light and magnetism, leading to a complete electromagnetic theory. This fitted in well with the then fashionable idea of an underlying luminiferous ether able to undulate.

At this point dynamics was invaded by statics. The success of relativity had demonstrated that the world was four-dimensional. The progress of a light signal became a diagonal line along the side of an imaginary cone. How then could the wave properties of light be reconciled? Analysis allowed only three real dimensions, so, as per relativity, time itself became imaginary. This error was continued as an imaginary space/time continuum replacing the ether. An empirical wave equation was devised to explain the behaviour of elementary particles—atoms, electrons, and even energy quanta. But the Shrödinger equation only dealt with abstractions, and its waves were only seen as rhythmic rises and declines in probabilities. It is conceded that, in this way, all the events and interactions of the physical world were brought together. But why are photons slowed down by transparent bodies? What is the rationale of reflection, refraction, interference, and the optical rotations? What is the electral picture of a quantum? To these questions wave mechanics could offer no simple, straight, or commonsense answers.

Chapter 9
Molecular Resonance

I sang of the dancing stars,
I sang of the daedal earth,
And of heaven and the giant wars,
And love, and death, and birth.
　　　　　—P. B. Shelley

The outstanding inferences from the correspondencies we have already observed and verified, i.e., those between electric force and gravity, electric charge and mass, X ray diffraction spacings, nuclear dimensions and Planck's constant (see Chapters 3, 5, 6, and 8) should have reconciled us to the idea that chemical molecules, i.e., all the ultimate particles of the physical and material universe, were once four-dimensional in character and structure. The only ostensible reason why they appeared to be three-dimensional arose from the universal Fitzgerald contraction generated by the big bang. This ubiquitous influence itself arose from supreme electric force.

The influx of energy arising from the big bang might have been sufficient momentarily to contract preexistent neutrons along the lines of their respective radiants. This contraction may have incidentally resulted in the generation of random electrons and energy quanta. In this way all atomic nuclei, protons, or neutrons could have momentarily lost a dimension. On the other hand, electrons and quanta may have behaved randomly because they simply filled in the space/time opened up· by the contraction. We might think that this almost instantaneous contraction might give rise to an equivalent recovery as the wave of time proceeded. Thus we come to the startling deduction that all moments in time spring back again into their natural four-dimensional form as the wave passes on. The transformation might occur rather like the momentary progress of the percussion wave along a line of shunted railway trucks. All this has fundamental implications regarding our own individual lives. Many poets and thinkers have observed the analogy of the progress of life with the weaving of a fabric, as in these lines from Blake.

> Joy and woe are woven fine,
> A clothing for the soul divine.

In our picture of creation as a wave, we are suggesting how this transformation of ourselves may come about. In Chapter 3, we saw how Fitzgerald's contraction could be seen as arising from Pythagoras. We could accept its three divisions as a unity, as we readily accept the three dimensions of space. But we could also see them as arising from the continuous, transverse penetration by "becoming" across a background surface of void. We may think of space as though it were a triple-ribbed umbrella. Closed, it signifies space as a single line; open, it becomes three lines, each at right angles to form the three spatial dimensions. But the stem of the umbrella remains to indicate the line of flow of time and the open whole typifies its dynamic arrowhead.

Earlier we saw how faith in atoms traces its origins far back into the mists of the past. When our primitive ancestors first learned how to crack a flint to get a sharp edge, they began a train of discontinuity leading to the atom. The passage of time and the unfolding of history act like the operation of a gigantic loom. The imperious clatter of shuttle and heddles corresponds with the clamourous and decisive present, and their swift actions contrast sharply with the slow let-off of the design. The construction of a fabric ultimately devolves to the manipulation of its individual warp and weft threads, and their line of synthesis corresponds with the sharp edges of hard objects: flints, jewels, metals, which led the Greeks to their atomic hypothesis. It is proposed to extend this argument to general existence: the present is a sharp edge, and our awareness of it means that spatiousness, together with the extensiveness of time, also comprise a grained structure. This is closely comparable with the individual warp and weft threads of a fabric, which form its essential background and fineness.

The void background of space/time may thus be made up of exceedingly tiny units, like atoms, but four-dimensional microhyperspheres, the micres we have already described. The hyper-ether formed from their assemblage may be able to embrace the truths of relativity and also those of quantum theory. When vector analysts talk of quanta, they quite naturally refer to the two essential, yet transverse vectors, electric and magnetic, which together activate electromagnetic radiation. The rays themselves proceed forward with the velocity of light, C. Their most essential wave nature follows as an unpredictable wave pattern. This unpredictability may arise because the oscillations could take place outside the plane of time. The rationale behind the analysis presupposes "least action," and shortly after Newton's death, De Maupertois introduced this extra-mechanical quality. It was defined as the product of momentum and distance—a wave of light was always supposed to be transmitted across the least distance between two points as a fundamental law. Energy became the rate of change of action, and its ultimate unit corresponded perfectly with Planck's constant, h. High frequency radiation should thus produce a high frequency of momenta, leading to the basic equation of the quantum theory:

$$(1), E = hV,$$
E, energy radiated per sec, V frequency, and h, Planck's constant.

We referred previously to attempts by both Eddington and Dirac to compare electric and gravitational forces acting side by side. We agreed that the constants for the proton were more reliable than those for the electron. The velocity and position of the latter was difficult to pin down. On the other hand, we could see the electron, circling as an eddy in four dimensions, as closely in keeping with this unreliability. These electronic eddies may be similar to those of a fast-flowing river. They appear and disappear randomly on the general suface, while the broader positive areas, where the water is rising, are more stable. The overall movement thus corresponds with the steady but refreshing flow of time. A similar allegory arises with the depressions and anticyclones of oncoming weather.

Positive Electricity: The Proton

Earlier we visualised an electron as an ultimate particle, spinning at peripheral velocity, C, distributed evenly around a ring, radius 0.705×10^{-13} cm. We should see the electron like a sphere, but showing an extra dimension, a hypersphere. Suppose a sphere were to spin at an ever higher and higher velocity, it would change eventually into a spinning ring, and this ring could go on accelerating until it reached the absolute, limiting, peripheral velocity, C. Imagine a similar sequence happening to a microhypersphere, a micre. The axis of the ring could be the fourth dimensional axis of time. We shall see later how this axial spin might induce a strongly future-past magnetic field. This could allow pairs of electrons strongly to attract each other, although otherwise repelled by their like electric charges.

Clearly, an electronic eddy may show two opposed, possible directions of spin, Z or S, corresponding with either a positron or an electron. But the preponderance of the latter, and the corresponding imbalance of parity, just as the imbalance of parity found by Lee and Yang for *pi* mesons, suggests a direction for the flow of time, in line with the temporal arrowhead of thermodynamics. If an electron may be a kind of eddy involving many micro-hyperspheres, then a single quantum could arise from the instantaneous activation of a single micre. The simplest nucleus, the proton itself, might be seen as the complete opposite of the electron. It might be an ultramicroscopic black hole, 0.705×10^{-13} cm in radius, sucking in micres in a directly opposite way to the divergent electron. It might thus provide the backlash to propel forward the progressive wave of time. Working together they could provide that intense pressure that brings all reality into being.

Perhaps we could think of micres rather like grains of sand. When we squeeze such a mass sufficiently the sand may cohere into a unified lump; clay does it even better because its particles are smaller. Similarly when many unit micres are sucked together by regression at C, they may be expected to cohere superficially by this "widdershin" spin. Should this intense pressure occur, it could result in two types of possible contortions: a shell effect causing gravitation and a bulk effect generating opposite electric charges. Force always arises from a direction outside and vertical to space/time. It is an expression of creative will and can never be absolutely predictable (see Introduction, p. 2). The space/time liberated by such a compression may thus appear as a negative zone, concentric with its nucleus. Newton proved long ago that a spherical shell behaved as though its attraction were situated at its centre; so that a particle with concentric opposite charges would appear neutral like a neutron. We may, therefore, reasonably expect that the pre-big bang, primeval mega-atom, lying like a seed or an egg in the midst of space/time, was composed of many neutrons. When it exploded, with the ebullition of immense energy, a fraction of this was converted to neutral hydrogen and dispersed far and wide in all directions. It is noteworthy that the mass of a neutron is slightly greater than that of its equivalent neutral hydrogen.

The Velocity of Light—C

This is the preeminent physical constant. Not only does it define the relation between space and time, it is also central to electromagnetic theory and relativity. For this reason, anything that threatens its credibility ought to be suspect. Yet when we examine the so-called laws of refraction arising from "least action," we find that this all-important constant is subject to diverse modification by a number of seemingly quite irrelevant conditions: temperature, density, molecular weight, and the atomic structure of transparent solids. Thus the velocity with which light is supposed to be propagated through a wide range of substances is supposed to be subject to a wide variation. Furthermore, lights of varying wavelengths, were said to proceed at greater or lesser velocities through any transparent solid, thus giving rise to the related phenomenon of optical dispersion. The velocity of light forms the lynchpin of astronomy. Astronomers often notice a reddening of the light from a distant galaxy or, more often, the alternations of redness and blueness from the light of a rapidly orbiting binary star. Yet these effects are ascribed respectively to the general recession of galaxies and the Doppler effect. No one suggests that these latter changes in wavelength are due to a slowing of the light. When Lord Rutherford in 1911 first directed alpha particles through a thin sheet of aluminium, he found that the spaces between atoms were mostly empty. In fact he extrapolated the size of a nucleus to be about 10^{-13} cm (see Chapter 6). How is it then that the empty spaces between atoms have a profound effect on light; while the empty spaces between stars have so little effect? The answer can only be that the collections of atoms we call molecules are really four-dimensional.

The electric and magnetic vectors of light are engaged in transverse oscillations; and these should have little effect on the forward motion of photons. We can only assume that they start out at C, and are much too small to be affected or slowed down by particles of less than atomic size. On the other hand we can readily see how the negative exteriors of photons may be guided into a curved path and attracted around positively charged atomic centres, so that, assuming progression at their maximum velocity, C, their paths will be that much longer across a transparent solid. In short, the photon will follow a longer, undulating path, but its actual velocity C will only appear to decrease.

Optical and Molecular Magnetic Rotations

It has long been known that asymmetric molecules rotate the planes of polarised light to the right or the left according to the S or Z twists of their respective mirror-image conformations. Wave mechanics sees an electron, and even photographs it, as a cloud of probabilities. How should we properly account for the rotations of the planes of polarised light? We may very easily imagine that the two vectoral oscillations, electric and magnetic from a monochromatic ray might reasonably find two alternative paths through a crystal structured from orderly atomic centres. In this way the polarised rays could be separated using a Nicol prism of Iceland spar. These polarised planes may be thought to resemble I bars, the steel girders used in architectural construction. When an I bar is bent, its planes are forced into a relative rotation. If we follow an I bar ray passing through an ordered system of atoms (a crystal), we can readily see that bending to and fro will take place, but that there will be no final exiting rotation from a symmetrical crystal. We have already seen how a photon may show a negative exterior and how it may be attracted by a positive nucleus. In any asymmetric molecule, the positions of its polar centres, although equivalent in polarity, are neither equally nor oppositely separated in space, so that the previous angular deviations do not cancel. Molecular magnetic rotation arises because the negative outer fringe of a photon behaves rather like an electron—they both follow a curved path when attracted by a magnet. Having now explained most of the well-known optical effects on the basis of a constant velocity for light and other E/M radiations, this seems to be more satisfactory than the supposition of a large number of intermediate and lesser velocities.

As photons pass from a vacuum to air, and on through ever denser media, so the deflection caused by their ever more frequent encounters with polar centres increases. As we noted in Chapter 6, even warm water may retain some order. But crystallization represents a greater step towards consolidation. A crystal cell may be a further step towards a more extensive molecule. When a photon enters a molecule, there may be three possibilities:

(1) It may be progressively deflected, with its energy levels reduced to the resonant frequency of the molecule. Examples: molecules with absorption bands, fluorescent compounds, and dyes.

(2) The energy of the photon may be taken up completely and converted into other forms of molecular energy—translational or vibrational. Examples: carbon black and graphite.

(3) It may be gradually deflected and acclimatised, so that it finally continues to cycle indefinitely within its domain. Thus it may take up an internal resonance in equilibrium with its environment. The evolution of this curious balance may eventually lead to the first signs of consciousness. Examples: living molecules, polynucleotides, proteins, and carbohydrates.

Before going on to consider this last case in more detail (see Chapter 10), we should outline the history and development of the lesser complicated resonant structures.

Molecular Resonance

Why was the concept of an unsaturated, six-membered carbon ring system formulated by Kekulé so important? Because it opened up organic chemistry and its rationale enormously, but it also engendered a great deal of controversy. This was because it upset previous thinking about the very foundations of the science. For example, the innumerable examples of compounds found in what was at first called "aromatic" chemistry, led on to almost equal numbers of possible isomers: compounds having the same ultimate composition, but otherwise showing great differences in their physical and chemical properties.

One great controversy centred on the term first used by chemists: dynamic isomerism. According to this, a compound might show the possibility of existing as two alternative structures, when only one could be actually prepared and produced. In some cases, two alternative forms of the same substance were actually prepared. Often one of these structures was coloured, while its congener was colourless. This state of affairs occurred with many dyestuffs, and the latter was called the benzenoid form, because benzene itself was colourless. The actual dye was called "quinonoid" because the substance, quinone was itself highly coloured; and it was known to have parallel double bonds inside its six-membered atomic ring. Kekule himself gave his benzene ring the form of a triethylenic hexagon:

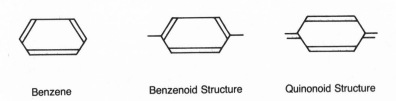

Benzene   Benzenoid Structure   Quinonoid Structure

Benzene, Benzenoid Structure, Quinonoid Structure

The benzene ring was greeted with much satisfaction at first. But when molecular symmetry demanded a whole brood of steric isomers that failed to materialise, the difficulty was overcome by imagining that in most cases the rate of alternation between isomers was too fast to allow isolation. The six equivalent hydrogens were thought to be engaged in a hectic molecular dance. This was not at all to the liking of physicists, who supposed that if electrons were able to move dynamically, then they should also be in process of generating observable E/M radiation.

Simultaneous with all the above chemical findings, there were vastly more spectacular discoveries being made in fundamental physics: electronic discharge in vacuo, cathode rays, positive rays, X rays, elementary radioactivity isotopes, and culminating with atomic fission and fusion. Clearly, everybody thought that physics had far outshone chemistry in importance. Wave mechanics itself produced ideas about the way two hydrogen atoms could join together to form a hydrogen molecule, H_2. How could two positively charged nuclei, each attended by a negatron, possibly join together to form the quite stable molecule of hydrogen? The mathematical physicists' answer was by the wave mechanical resonance between the two electrons. Not resonance in the direct sense of the term—reinforced beats—but a resonance of probabilities. The true meaning of resonance implies reinforced beats: reinforcement. Force itself is defined by electrons. And we have seen that these are four-dimensional: three in space and one in time. Reality is four-dimensional.

What has all the above got to do with chemistry and its most important link, the co-valent bond? We have to discover the rationale of two similarly charged electrons coming together by some kind of attraction. In fact this can only be magnetic. We saw in Chapters 3, 5, 6 and 8, how electrons might be engaged in spinning at C, along the perimeter of a minute ring. How could a four-dimensional electron possibly get into a two-dimensional ring? First because it was originally shot off at C by the big bang; and in the second place because it achieved its ultimate angular velocity by being spun at peripheral speed C about an axis along the direction of time. It is noteworthy that although helium, the alpha particle, has four times the mass of a proton, yet its boiling point is 16.2 degrees centigrade lower than that of hydrogen, and that it has not as yet been changed into a solid. These findings agree with the idea that helium holds a structure more inert and condensed than any other element. This could arise because its atom is held together, not only by its two positive charges, but also by its two electrons, which also cling to each other additionally by virtue of the maximum magnetic force.

Chapter 10

Living Molecules

Be careful as you walk the street,
Not to step on a germ in embryo sweet,
Which might culminate in a man,
By the great Darwinian Theory.
—Anonymous, *Scottish Students' Song-book*

The resonance of simple compounds, such as benzene and water may reveal a lot about the larger, often linear, molecules that make up the fibrous structures of plants and animals. One outstanding feature of resonance is its tendency to behave unpredictably. For example: the first two members of the oxygen family of the elements are oxygen and sulphur. And the latter's atom is twice as heavy as the former's. Further, oxygen is known to be a life-giving gas, while sulphur is a compact yellow solid. If anyone were predicting, without actual experience, what the respective normal hydrides might be like, one would naturally imagine that the hydride of oxygen should be a gas, following its parents, whereas one might think that that of sulphur could be anything. In fact it is the other way round. Hydrogen sulphide is the gas and water is the very extraordinary liquid.

Water is unpredictable because of its resonance. Its molecules join together into many types of aggregate. Commonly known as H_2O, it should be seen as a resonance-bonded polymer $(H_2O)_n$. The complexity and multiplicity of form of ice crystals and snowflakes are due to resonance. But if the resonance is eliminated by the addition of sufficient salt, the product (brine) is considered sterile, like the waters of the Dead Sea. Brine is often used as an antiseptic or preservative. We should always be careful when we use the adjective *living*. About one hundred years ago when biological evolution was beginning to come to the fore, both Darwin and Russell Wallace conceived the idea that there should be a minimum starting point for all biology; a unicellular organism, an amoeba, or even a single yeast cell. These early pioneer biologists were mainly concerned with fossil remains discovered in rocks whose formation eras might be geologically and biologically estimated and verified. This was the only way the budding theory of evolution could be firmly established. They left the more difficult question of the prior origin and evolution of their single-celled organisms for future consideration. In those early days, exact knowledge about the age of the Earth as a planet was an astronomical mystery. Somewhat later Lord Kelvin roughly estimated from thermodynamics and cooling that the sun might have taken fifteen million years to achieve its present heat. This figure was far less than the hundreds of millions of years estimated by geological and biological research.

It was only when the importance of nuclear energy, as a source of solar and stellar radiation, was realised that the period times for biological and geological evolution began to fit in with astronomical estimates. For example, the age of the Sun was later estimated as about 6,000 million years, and that of the Earth as 4,500 million years; while the time lapsed since the big bang is more accurately estimated as 20,000 million years. The period back to the earliest fossils became 1,000 million years. These times are important because, although the latter, i.e., that from unicellular units to man, seems incredibly long, yet the prior evolution of the unit cell from resonant molecules is even more difficult to properly comprehend. We have to remember that even the unit cell is a sophisticated complex of minutely delegated activity compared with a relatively simple virus particle. Yet even a virus has a double-chain of DNA sections, more elongated in proportion than an Atlantic cable. Certainly the 3,000 million years of evolution, which we know nothing about, may have closed a stupendous gap of apparently unifying organisation by the transition from simple molecules to polypeptides, and from polypeptides to proteins, with the latter's incredible chains involving twenty-two diverse alpha-aminoacids.

Nature's Helical Design

What are the three main fibrous structures that underlie the living world; and what do they have in common? First, there is the polynucleotide helix, composed of dual and vastly elongated chains of DNAs. DNA is cryptic for deoxyribonucleic acid. Ribose is a curious pentose found in currants ("ribes"). Ribose ($C_5 H_{10} O_5$) has five carbon atoms to its ring, and is otherwise quite like another well-known hexose—glucose ($C_6H_{12}O_6$) with six carbon atoms to its ring. The double DNA became famous because it encapsulates the hereditary code for its parent organism. Multicellular organisms form communities of cells cooperating together as though they formed a single individual, and every unit cell of the organism has a helical chain of DNA that determines its cellular character. All living creatures grow by cell division, and when a cell divides, its double strand of DNA separates, and each divided strand forms a template, which directs and determines the character of its dual partner in the proces of formation. The most functional parts of the DNA chain are the resonance bonds, which link between its two pairs of complementary bases.

Most people think of their physical bodies as harmonised collections of muscles, nerves, veins, glands, arteries, et cetera, which all work together to keep their physique in good order. But all this complex organisation is rather like a quiet, private, and personal civil service. It carries on mainly to keep everything normal and viable. Few people are aware that there must be an underlying duplicate, yet much more delicately balanced organisation, also forever at work, keeping everything calm and normal, yet in a proper and persistent equilibrium. The question is: What is the physical basis for this subtle, underlying, but more fundamental service? Our minds? Are we ourselves made up of two parts, physical and mental? If there is a mind as well as a body, how and why does it seem to function independently? The complexity of one human being is enormously amplified by a big city. We come again to the problem of thought and decision. Local civil services keep traffic, water, and power supplies moving smoothly, but only according to plan. We are trying to suggest that thought may basically arise at a deep molecular level, not from the bloodstream or from the nervous system, but more fundamentally from electromagnetic resonance, and that electricity is the driving force behind this resonance. We know that force is generated by acceleration, and acceleration itself comes from a change of tempo. In other words, human *will*, a change of tempo, only arises from outside the plane of space and time.

Although nearly everyone has heard about the double DNA helix, fewer know of another earlier helix conceived by the famous chemist Linus Pauling. The Pauling alpha helix was conceived to account for the remarkable elasticity of wool and other protein fibres. The great point about Pauling's helix is that it unfolds out from its coiled alpha form and takes up a straighter configuration, the beta form. The peptide links that make up the structure of the wool protein, keratin, also show a remarkable cross-resonance. This allows them to link together along the line of the lengthy chains. Resonance follows the peptide link, and may allow a concerted influence to proceed, to remain in harmony with an animal's whole structure. People often make the remark: "I felt it with every fibre of my being," by which they are commenting on their nervous reaction to an idea.

Everyone knows about their immediate nervous system, with its network of minute veins, arteries, and blood supply. What is more reluctantly conceded is that there exists any other, finer, and more delicate mechanism, constantly in operation, and which also defines the feat of being alive. How is this resonance relayed, and particularly what happens when the effect comes to a dead-end, when a fibre tapers off and finishes? Here a possible clue is provided by what have become known as the "essential aminoacids." It is accepted that there are about twenty-two different aminoacids, which make up the structures of proteins. But there is also a smaller group, notably phenylalanine, tyrosine, and tyrptophane, all derived alpha, amino propionic acids, which are essential for the proper nutrition of an animal. It is surprising that while the subject of nutrition is well publicised, some important aspects are some-

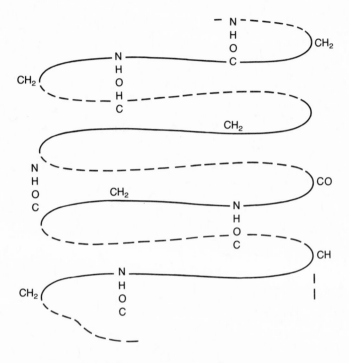

Figure 1. Resonance Bonds along the Pauling Helix

times passed over. For example, everyone knows that there are three classes of essential foods: carbohydrates, fats, and proteins. What is rarely mentioned is that proteins go through a complex preliminary hydrolysis on assimilation. They break down into their respective acids, and if the digesting animal is short of one essential, it picks out this residue, and allows the remainder to follow their less important function of supplying energy. It is not stressed that anyone can subsist on relatively less protein, given ample carbohydrate and fat, because the required amount of the essential acid may be only a small fraction of the protein.

The principle was captured a hundred years ago by Marie Lloyd, with her song: "A little bit of what you fancy does you good."

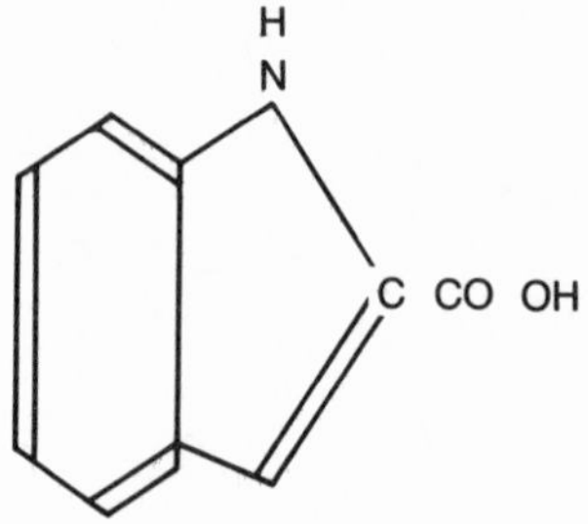

Tryptophane

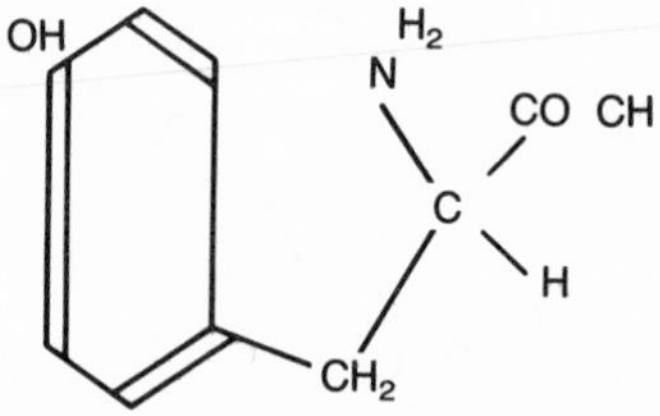

Tyrosine

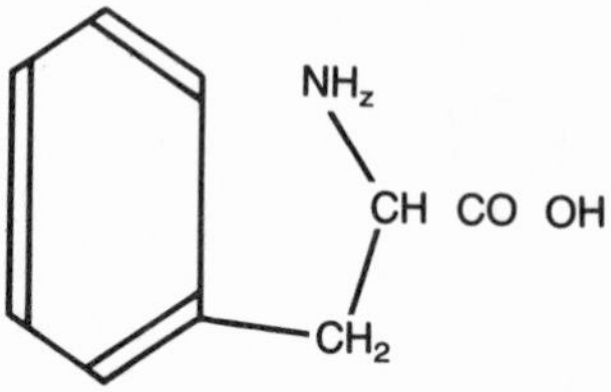

Phenylalanine: phenylamino-propionic acid

Figure 2. Similarities of Structure between the Three Essential Amino Acids

It is underlined by the well-known fastidiousness of pregnant women. Even rats will discriminate between foods, when in need of some essential item. They all comprise unsaturated ring structures and incipient indole rings. We might imagine that these ring combinations might be just the ones to provide an outstanding resonance. They also show the possibility of outstanding physiological effects. Why should an unsaturated ring affect the longer resonance of a peptide chain? We might think of the possibility of photon reflection as by a parabolic mirror. The biological resonance might proceed along the exterior peptide links of helices and along the fibre axis. When the effect reached a ring structure, its direction might be reversed through 180 degrees of arc, giving a rationale for low-frequency oscillation. What might we surmise about such a possible wave? Firstly that its energy is likely to show a lower frequency than that of visible light. One can be easily misled regarding the wave energy of infrared light. Because radiant energy naturally feels nice and warm, and also because a lot of people nowadays actually cook in radiofrequency ovens, we are apt to think that the individual waves are more energetic, whereas, of course, they are proportionally less so. When we come to living waves, their slight effects may well explain why they have not as yet been physically demonstrated. The life process probably began with the plant kingdom. Chlorophyll, with its special structure of eight unsaturated rings encasing a magnesium atom, is responsible for photosynthesis and the basic food supply of most living creatures. Both the central magnesium atom and its eight-satellite unsaturated rings are capable of resonance. It is pertinent that the chlorophyll absorbs light from the red and orange end of the solar spectrum; while its bright green yellow shade show that it is rejecting the shorter wavelengths. About forty years ago Russian scientists claimed effects of what they called "mitogenic radiation," said to be emitted when cells were undergoing division (mitosis); but little has been heard recently about this. Cellulose is the third helical long-chain, living molecule; and chlorophyll may focus its energy.

There is an important, connected problem in biology: What ought we to take as the unit of certain species of insect? The bee or its hive, the ant or the anthill? It has been noticed that even single-celled plants, such as yeast, seem to show a tendency to form colonies. It may be that the future holds further advances in the sensitivity of detection. The well-known tendency for individual animals to associate together and to form a herd is so widespread and deep-seated, that it demands some direct channel of action. This could be provided by a further study of resonance bonding. The DNA helix is recognised mainly as a store of information. Genes are not direct instruments of immediate action; they mostly perform a hereditary purpose. A further pointer is the resonance of water. Spring water was, and still is, traditionally obtained from a well. The word *well* itself has an interesting derivation. It is identical in Old English with *will*: which means having a strong spirit; welling or bubbling with enthusiasm. It has been known for ages that some people have the gift of water divining; which largely applies to running underground water. No physical connection between the diviner and the water has ever been demonstrated. But in this and many similar cases, there seems to be some influence that is transmitted across space and time without any apparently connected physical channel of action. We can only surmise that this channel may be unseen, because it never actually lies in the plane of space/time. Yet it repeatedly crosses the plane through an extra depth of being.

Memory and Resonance*

One of the most fascinating and mysterious aspects of the human mind is the faculty of memory. When it became possible to track down and check the various functions of the brain, it naturally seemed feasible that the extensive frontal lobes might contain a zone where memories could be stored. Karl Lashley made prodigious efforts to check this, but could not pin down a specific area. It seemed from his results that learning could occur almost anywhere and everywhere.

In recent times the brain has been likened to a computer. Both

*R. L. Wormell, "Memory and Hydrogen Bonding," *Chemistry in Britain*, vol. 10, no. 2 (February 1974): 63.

comprise arrangements of many subunits, cf neurons and transistors; both show complex interconnections, of nerves and wires. But in sharp contrast, a computer is generally connected to an extensive memory bank; whereas, in the brain, memory has been shown to be associated with chemical changes. Once, it was even claimed that actual molecules carrying learned information could be fed or injected from one animal to another; and there was the well publicised experiment of teaching flatworms by feeding them with the remains of other well-educated flatworms.

What is more difficult to understand is the great volume of possible human memories:

> And still they gazed, and still the wonder grew,
> That one small head could carry all he knew.

Freud likened the subconscious to the submerged nine-tenths of an iceberg; but even this estimate may be far too low. In his remembrances of things past Marcel Proust described how dunking a bit of Madeleine cake in a cup of coffee revived a whole book of memories. It seems incredible that the host of possible associations, both conscious and subconscious, could all exist materially and be codified by specific protein chains; yet there must be some mechanism that allows us to delve into the past and bring back to life events that might have been considered lost for ever.

One factor in memory that has not been given the consideration it deserves is resonance bonding. Inheritance identified in genes is really an extreme case of race memory, where characters are passed on through the very accurate copying of a pattern accomplished by hydrogen bonding across the double helix of DNA. The fact that the RNA content of the brain rises with learning could mean that it forms resonance bonds with protein in a definite coded pattern, thus forming a transcribed copy of what is being learned. Messenger RNA has to move freely inside the cell; and in so doing, it continuously encounters protein molecules and could be slightly modified and retain imprints. RNA wandering through the cell could also account for the holographic aspect of memory. Every protein molecule in the brain could thus retain imprints of passing RNAs.

*In New Fibres from Proteins,** a theory of protein structure was outlined, which drew a parallel between the micellae of cellulose and the giant corpuscular molecules of the proteins. There was a duality in protein structure that reconciled basic polypeptide chains with the possibility of interchain connections to produce unit corpuscles. These could expose extensive surfaces, and the inception of the Pauling alpha helix revealed an interconnecting system of resonance bonds on the helical surfaces. How could any message, typified by a specific sequence of RNA bases be transferred to the resonance-bonded corpuscular surface as a related pattern of modified bonds?

The credibility of just such a process is strengthened by a repeatable experiment using readily available and less complicated material. During the early 1920s a new type of cellulosic fibre was developed in which cellulose molecules were first fully acetylated and then allowed to ripen or hydrolyse until they became perfectly acetone-soluble by conversion into a secondary acetate. A viscous dispersion of the ester was then extruded and shaped into filaments by an evaporative technique. At first, some difficulty was experienced in dyeing the new fibres; but later a range of dyestuffs specific to cellulose esters was developed. At the time it seemed surprising that the ester was not susceptible to the already well-established direct dyes used for cotton goods, because the ripening process was supposed to set free hydroxyl groups—certainly the secondary ester showed physical properties quite different from the original triactetate, whose lack of active centres for resonance bonding had conferred a hydrophobic quality.

Dyeing experience with the new secondary fibres later brought to light a curious property. If the material were creased or pressed prior to dyeing with direct dyes, the crease subsequently developed as a coloured line. In fact it was proposed at the time to exploit such a procedure as a method of embossing designs, pictures, et cetera. The rationale of the effect was then ascribed to a slight displacement or activation of latent resonance bonds in the fibre. A fabric so treated is superficially identical with the "grey" (fresh

*R. L. Wormell, *New Fibres from Proteins* (London: Butterworths, 1954).

from the loom); and it seems to have "remembered" its past treatment. Thus it is feasible that a similar modified resonance bonding in the brain could be responsible for the revival of long-dimmed memories.

Having now reached the best point to recapitulate, we hope we have found unity from a wide assemblage. We first explained how time itself came into space and being as a wave; how this wave solved most of the outstanding puzzles of astronomy; how dynamics led on to acceleration, and further, to mental decision as the director of force; how there was only one basic force that was essentially electric; and even gravitation and the mysterious Fitzgerald contraction, were essentially electric. There is a mental attitude known as *holism*; which gave rise to holistic medicine. It springs from the belief that a healthy person should be whole; a wholeman whole. We hope we have established something of the holism of science. It is important because it can give us all tremendous hope and relaxation, and a positive attitude to life. Shakespeare

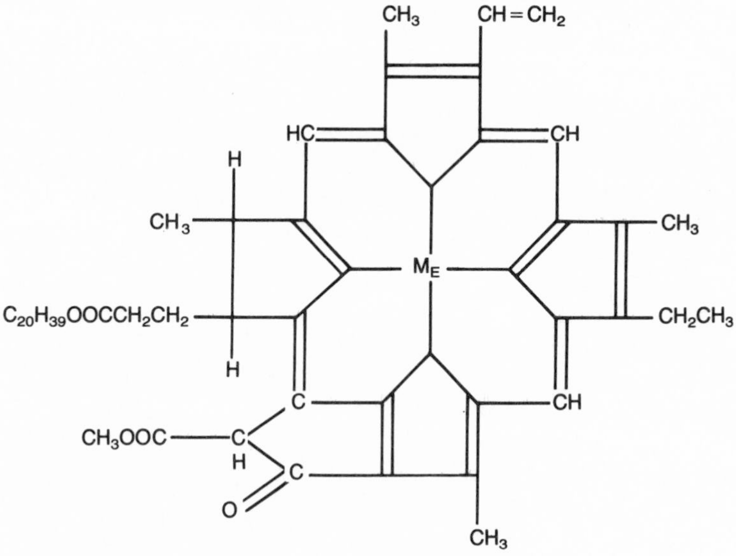

Figure 3. The Structure of Chlorophyll

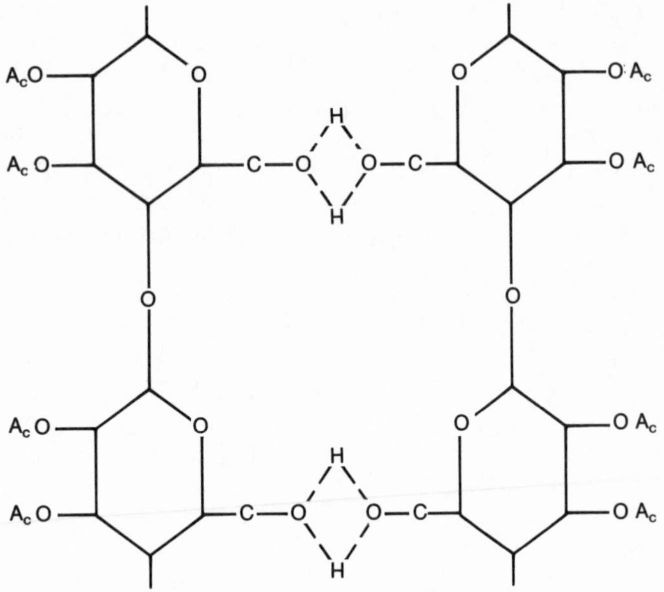

Figure 4. Resonance Bonds in Secondary Cellulose Acetate

and his works were built around the holism of Aristotle. Newton's dynamics was built from his belief in the unity of God. We believe that, even today, we can only get peace of mind by seeing the universe as a supreme, living, and evolving unity.

Chapter 11

The Corpuscular Theory of Proteins

God in the First Creation made atoms.
    —Isaac Newton

I first began to study proteins during the rise of Mussolini during the late twenties and early thirties. Italy at that time was very short of foreign currency, especially sterling. Yet Italy was in possession of extensive agricultural areas, notably on the southern slopes of its Northern Alps. These lands were mostly devoted to cattle and their many dairy products. The firm to which I was then engaged, Courtauld's Ltd., was then allied to a subsidiary company; Snia Viscosa, which produced Italian viscose fibres. An Italian chemical engineer, Antonio Ferretti, conceived the original idea that he could draw fibres from milk casein, the main protein of milk, by a process similar to the extrusion of cellulose xanthate from wood pulp. It was a perceptive and original step. After all, cellulose dispersions were similar to casein, in that both were soluble in alkalies. Cellulose formed sodium xanthate and casein formed sodium caseinate. Both solutions attained a viscosity suitable for extrusion; they both pulled out and set between the fingers into simulated fibre. Ferretti was the first to extrude commercially regenerated protein fibres, and the product was called Lanital, Italian wool.

Many critics of the Ferretti process said that "If Italy had any surplus milk, it ought to be used to feed their starving babies," rather than to be devoted to the production of a shoddy, imitation wool. But more careful consideration established that there were times on the prairies of America, the Pampas of Argentina and in

New Zealand, when Spring rains caused a sudden burgeoning of grass, which herds of cows obediently turned into milk. Of course, it is easy to pass this flush through centrifuges and produce a proportionate supply of cream. But this leaves over a large residue of skimmed milk, which can also be readily converted into edible cheese, yet the process has to be carefully controlled if it is to give a product fit for human consumption. It is much easier, in hot climates especially, to simply allow the milk to sour, preferably by the injection of a little suitable starter from a previous batch. The casein precipitates as curds, which are very easily separated and dried. Self-soured casein powder is a fairly available raw material. Because it is essentially acidic, it can be dissolved in dilute ammonia or other alkali, to produce spinnable dopes that give out fibres similar to rayon. By careful after-treatment of the fibres, their long molecular chains can be linked together using formaldehyde or other agents. Then by a progressive sequence of stretching, further hardening and stretching, their physical properties are greatly improved, giving a product comparable to wool.

The discoveries of Ferretti were well publicised; but mainly to advertise how well the Axis powers could get on by the clever adaptation of their self-sufficient economies. Thus it was not very surprising when three eminent university professors, all Fellows of the Royal Society: Astbury, Chibnall, and Bailey applied for a patent for making textile fibres from peanuts and other vegetable proteins. The patent was later taken over and developed by I.C.I. Ltd; and the product was called Ardil, since it was produced at Ardeer, Ayr, Scotland, the headquarters of the Nobel Explosive Industries. The directors of Courtaulds were somewhat annoyed that Astbury had bypassed them, and gone straight to the top: to the British chemical giant, I.C.I. From its early days, Courtaulds had long enjoyed a gentleman's agreement with I.C.I., according to which they would not invade I.C.I. preserves regarding sulphuric acid, if I.C.I. would, *pari passu*, keep away from rayon.

From the start, Ardil was conceived on the basis of Prof. Astbury's researches on the X-ray structures of fibrous proteins. He was deeply committed to X-ray analysis, after his collaboration with Professor Sir Lawrence Bragg. Astbury had published an illuminating and successful book; *The Fundamentals of Fibre Structure.* I had read this book with alacrity; it seemed to open up a wide vista for further investigation. Astbury's picture of the alpha and beta chains of wool-keratin showed that the former was simply a folded form of the latter. Wool was similar in aminoacid composition to all the other proteins, and it was logical to suppose that all native protein macromolecules might comprise long, but folded polypeptide chains. If these were dispersed in a suitable solvent, then according to X-rays, there was every reason to believe that, after appropriate stretching, they would straighten and line up to give a product showing some of the splendid properties of wool and silk. It was a fair ambition.

The first step was to find a suitable yet mild dispersing agent. What could be more suitable than urea, the nitrogenous end-product of biological metabolism? I suppose Astbury tried aqueous urea, and found that it gave a suitably viscous and fibre-forming sticky mass. After that I think he consulted Professors Chibnall and Bailey about the possibilities of carefully extracting proteins from native seeds. They decided that peanuts were the most suitable and available raw material. Films of the dispersed protein were coagulated in salty, acid baths, and when positive results were obtained, the process was covered by patents. Later it was passed on to Messrs. I.C.I. for development. All these native seed products were thought to have developed in a globular form. They should be very carefully extracted at relatively low pH to prevent premature denaturation. Astbury regarded a native protein molecule as though it were a miniature, rolled-up ball of woollen-spun yarn. He was anxious not to disturb their ordered folded regularity. For this reason special autoclaves were produced to enable the meal, after pressing to remove extraneous oil, to be finally oil-extracted using low-boiling hydrocarbons—hexane or pentane. Then the residual hydrocarbons could themselves be removed by applying vacua at low temperature. It was all costly and long-winded. We found at Courtaulds that better fibres, although at the cost of a slightly lower yield, could be made by using ordinary commercial cattle-cake, extracted by using the usual solvents at 120°C. The material was then finally dispersed using 1 percent caustic soda.

The great drawback in using urea as a basic dispersing agent is that it is too organically reactive. It happens to be the starting point for a whole class of plastics: the urea-formaldehyde resins, so that when formaldehyde was added to the spinning bath, this became cluttered with a miasma of insoluble particles: Goldschmidt's compound. Even if there had been no formalin present on spinning, the fibres would have had to be extracted to remove excess urea before proceeding. In practice Messrs. I.C.I. soon adopted dilute caustic soda for dispersion. For several years, I was suitably impressed with Astbury's general ideas about lining up the long protein chains. We tried all possible variations of coagulation, prehardening, stretching, and final hardening. In this way we produced quite practicable textile products. Such materials might have been very acceptable to Courtaulds during the period preceding World War II, because they could have been blended with viscose "Fibro," then already in competition with cotton. A blend of completely man-made fibres, with similar properties to those of the "Vyella" type, might then have been very popular.

With the advent of the war, I was thirty-eight years old, and I was reserved from the services by Courtaulds. A certain amount of research on protein fibres (Fibrolane) was carried out in spite of air raids, and other higher priority efforts. After the war the outlook had changed considerably because of the appearance of totally synthetic fibres. These products followed on from the success of nylon, "Orlon" from acetylene and "Terylene" from coal tar intermediates. The synthetics, apart from being something quite new and unexpected, were much more tenacious, elastic, and stable than the traditional natural fibres, and in this way, enjoyed a considerable vogue. Nevertheless, in the years succeeding the war, an improved pilot plant for casein fibres was erected. For a time this secured profitable outlets. In addition, Courtaulds was now prepared to spend a lot more on research and development. A new X-ray department was set up, in the charge of Dr. F. Happey, who had previously assisted Professor Astbury at Leeds University.

When various proteins from milk and seeds were subject to X-rays, their plates all showed an even ring. This confirmed Astbury's finding that fibrous proteins were structured from lengthy polypeptide chains. The great hope was to stretch out the extruded and hardened fibres to get some added information as a pattern of X-ray spots. These tests were only partially successful. Besides confirming the presence of main chains, it became possible to concentrate their rings into spots on their equators. But no sharply detailed, X-ray pictures, such as have been found with natural silk and other highly stretched cellulose and synthetic fibres were obtained. Yet the transformation of structure between alpha and beta-keratin was confirmed. More particularly, an important reflection showing a 1.5 Å spacing for the alpha form, endorsed the reality of Pauling's alpha helix. We saw in Chapter 10 that this led on to views about resonance that may be fundamentally valuable.

As regards regenerated proteins, however, nothing exceptionable could be observed. Dr. Happey revealed that our best fibres were only about 30% in line; the rest of the structure appeared amorphous.

These findings caused me to change my basic picture; to bring it into line with the micelle theory; and general experience with textile fibres (see p. 22, *New Fibres from Proteins*,). When you consider the 22–23 possible alpha aminoacids, they appear a very awkward squad. Only glycine is symmetrical. It is not surprising, in view of the bulk and multiplicity of their side chains, that the X-ray negatives from regenerated casein show a common background of fog. I eventually came round to the view that soluble protein molecules were essentially globular. Their extruded fibres hung together rather like beads on a string. Naturally this was not at all to the liking of Professor Astbury. He had adopted a rather glamorous picture of proteins. Thus he had a suit made of Ardil, and at a time shortly before the exposure of the futilities of the Ground-nut Scheme for Africa, he went on television to proclaim his exciting ideas.

The African Ground-nut Scheme

At the time, I went to hear a lecture about this, given at the Royal Society of Arts, South Kensington, London. This was an imaginative and ingenious plan. It was, like Astbury's structural ideas, a bit top-heavy with *a priori* theory. Using a large map of Africa, the lecturer outlined the area devoted to the scheme. Thus it appeared, amid the vastness, only like one of the square black dots used to denote capital cities. In fact, it was a pilot scheme that might have revolutionised the food production of the Dark Continent. But it failed for a variety of reasons. For example, although the annual rainfall for the area was about the same average as for the British Isles, it came in dollops rather than as drips and drops. Thus there were places in the included area that had had no rain for three years. Superficially the African interior is rather like California in its covered-wagon days, with its Death Valley, Cottonwoods, and Funeral Mountains. Today much of the western side of America has blossomed and become comfortable because of water conservation and irrigation. The Ground-nut Scheme was ahead of its time. One great deficiency was the lack of proper defence against the tsetse fly as a carrier of yellow fever. The fly is difficult to eradicate because of the extensive areas of bush that harboured wild fauna in spite of insecticides. Another reason for failure was the problem of servicing the secondhand tractors used.

Astbury was sent *New Fibres From Proteins* to review (*Science Progress*, 1956). He naturally seized on the X-ray pictures as his target. His main claim was that they were not consistent with basic science. All this, in spite of their not being the actual negatives, which X-ray experts insist are absolutely indispensable. I am not an X-ray expert and I personally disclaim total responsibility for their interpretation. All that I can say is that they were produced using his technique. Professor Astbury died shortly afterwards; and I refrained from polemics. Perhaps restraint was right, because nothing resolves factual disputes better than the lapse of time. Not long after, I.C.I. gave up the Ardil process, and regenerated protein fibres are not now in production. The dream of orientated products closely structured on wool and silk has vanished. This does not mean that man-made protein fibres may never reappear. They may come back as a blend with "noil," as an improved felt with leatherlike properties. Or even as warm fabrics, that are very kind to the touch. I believe that the comparatively minor defect of low resistance to hot acid dye baths will be overcome; possibly by the use of an agent such as ethylene oxide, which is able to neutralise most sidechain terminals. The oxide was very exotic in 1950, but today it is in everyday use.

I was not depressed by Astbury's inane review. Because of my job, I had lots of other things on my mind; but I do deplore the herd instinct shown by the leaders of science. I first conceived the idea of the "expanding universe" in 1950.* Before that (1916), I kept up with the latest views on cosmology, beginning with *Man's Place in the Universe* by Alfred Russell Wallace. I particularly read later popular accounts, such as Jean's *Mysterious Universe*, and *The Nature of the Physical World* by Eddington.

The only real test of any idea or theory is how it stands up to the test of time. I am glad to say that *Science and the Subjective* stands up pretty well. But later, when I contributed an article: "Memory and Hydrogen Bonding," to *Chemistry in Britain* (see Chapter 10), the editor warned me that the topic had previously incited heated argument. In sharp contrast, I have not received a word of comment from pundits. The worst fate of any innovator is to be ignored. I hope I qualify as someone with ideas. In 1924 I was awarded the Discussion Prize at Birmingham University's Chemical Society.

I feel that there was, in my time, a condescending and snobbish attitude taken to applied research in contrast to that brought to the academic. A colleague of mine described it as emanating from "A trades union of University Professors." Not so long ago, British society was worm-eaten with class distinctions; more especially in its lower grades. Why is the corpuscular theory of proteins important to the the unity of the universe? Because it emphasises the binding role of resonance in the beta, peptide structure of the native proteins. These are the most significant molecules of organic chemistry. As we have seen in the preceding chapters, the universe is undulant, but its waves are tangible, physical waves. They are not fictitious ideas in the minds of theoreticians. The classic scientific rule for research and progress follows this sequence: experiment, observation, and inference. Yet even eminent people start the other

---

Science and the Subjective, s 16, C34, R.R.I, Winfield, B.C., Can. VOH 2CO.

way round. They theorise before doing tests. We have seen how a mountain of theory has been built around the idea of "action." Action is defined as being the product of work and time: dimensions ML^2T^{-1}. Thus L denotes two transverse lengths forming an area. But how can any one object move along two lengths at right angles at one and the same time? The whole concept is a figment of the imagination.

We saw earlier how Astbury had theorised about protein spinning prior to actually doing experiments. Incidentally when we ourselves were using extrusion baths containing formaldehyde, it was necessary to provide effective ventilation for operatives picking up the ends from the baths. This was done by using exhaust fans fixed above the surface of the liquid. An immediate problem was taking care of the pungent effluent air. Here was a case of experiment providing the clue to a much greater, worldwide problem: that of acid rain. We thought of available agents that could well deaden acid and formaldehyde. In this way we tried just a trickle of ammonia gas up a 100 foot stack. This immediately worked very well. The plant was situated in a residential area, an old excise warehouse from the days when rayon was taxed. The plant ran for about ten years without a single complaint, or a visible sign of the hexamine that must have been produced. When I finally left Courtaulds, I went on to do part-time teaching. I then instructed pupils about a way of eliminating sulphur dioxide from air; which even in those days (1960) was a problem by-product of electricity generation. I wrote to my M. P., who contacted Mr. Richard Crossman, then minister for the environment, and I was given an invitation to Warren Springs, then a large new laboratory for eliminating pollution.

A Simple Way of Defeating Acid Rain

Most fuels used for raising steam are likely to contain about 0.2 to 2% of sulphur. This latter is oxidised in furnaces to be converted into sulphur dioxide or trioxide; its ultimate fate being sulphuric acid. This is the originator, along with oxides of nitrogen and burnt P.V.C., of the acid rain so objectionable in the environment.

OUTLINE OF PROPOSED PROCESS

It is proposed to bleed the appropriate trickle of ammonia gas into the burnt effluent, flue gas, thereby neutralising the acidity and converting it into ammonium salts beneficial to plants and other kinds of vegetable life.

PROVISION OF AMMONIA GAS

The liquified gas may be purchased cheaply in cylinders. It can also be made quite simply from the nitrogen in the air and from hydrogen arising from the electrolysis of water. Nitrogen may be obtained by the fractionation of liquid air, or bought cheaply from plants producing oxygen. The two gases, nitrogen and hydrogen, combine under pressure at a raised temperature with the evolution of heat.

ADVANTAGES OF THE PROCESS

The ammonia gas mixes radidly with the turbulent effluent, and rises at high speed (about 60 mph) up the stack. Practically no ancillary plant for pumping liquids, spraying, scrubbing, and renewing solids, such as lime, is required. The products of the process, only a slight percentage, move into the atmosphere and are naturally deposited in rain to the benefit of all plant life in the environment. In pre-WWI days, ammonia was always a slight constituent of air. It arose from the horse manure than so prevalent. Decomposition of urea gave ammonia and CO_2. The former, being lighter, arose in the air. Thus the above process only replaces something lost. In fact the concentration of ammonia could be further increased to neutralise all the acidity of flue gases, motor exhausts, etc. Carbon dioxide would thus be converted into ammonium carbonate, and later to carbamate, halfway to carbamide (urea). In this way carbon dioxide might be cleared from air, to avoid the 'Greenhouse' effect, which is becoming ever more threatening.

I had a discussion with the officers there. They saw my point to some extent and agreed to do some laboratory tests. It was then found that ammonia did, in fact, react with sulphur dioxide to form ammonium sulphite. Correspondence continued for about two years, and a fat file built up. By this time the government had decided to build a series of five hundred-foot chimneys to disperse the oxide at high altitude. It was calculated that the large volume of rising air would actually reach a speed of 60 mph up the stacks. These high chimneys were to be built in the Trent Valley, where a series of large power stations using coal from the local Yorks and Notts coal fields were to be erected.

With this decision my scheme lost its impetus. Warren Springs was the direct successor to the Alkali Inspectorate. This government department was set up 150 years ago, to deal with the disgusting state of the river Mersey, Lancashire. A great stench periodically arose when both calcium sulphide and hydrochloric acid were dumped together into the water. This naturally produced the highly toxic hydrogen sulphide gas. Ironically the eventual value of the sulphur and salt by-products thus produced saved the old Le Blanc process from going out of production! The Inspectorate seemed to have accumulated, over the years, all the characteristics of a tired old watchdog, whose teeth had become a little soft. The results of the Warren Spring tests were not published, and the experts greatly magnified the difficulties of ammonia injection.

Shortly after this Mr. Crossman died. Then, a little later, the Labour Government went out of office. I again wrote to my new Conservative M.P., Mr. Butcher, who had also become a new junior minister, about acid rain. He also was quite cooperative. On this occasion the experts, advising the new minister for the environment, Mr. Waldegrave, made a great fuss about the imaginary clouds of ammonium sulphite particles, which they imagined would be showered on the immediate neighbourhoods. On the contrary,

I believed that these fears were quite groundless, because of the vast quantity of air rising at high speed in the stacks. Normally, clouds of steam are formed at conventional stations. But not until the effluent has risen four to five thousand feet into the air. Indeed the clouds are so self-adherent that they reach across the North Sea to Scandinavia, where they are said to cause a whole load of trouble. Unfortunately no real experimentation with ammonia injection has ever been carried out. The powers that be have thought about my scheme, but rejected it out of their heads and through their hats. Not only Warren Springs, but also the Central Electricity Generating Board were both dead against the innovation. It forms another example to add to the firm believers in "Action," and to Astbury's faith in urea, of mistaken *a priori* thinking.

Chapter 12

Relativity and Wave Mechanics Simplified

Elegance of presentation ought to be left to the tailors and cobblers.
—Albert Einstein

The relation (I) $E = mC^2$ is the outstanding contribution of relativity. Some rather overpositive claims were originally included with the theory.* Thus the derivation of the Fitzgerald-Lorentz contraction was achieved by equating nothing with nothing. The cardinal dimension of time was taken to be simply a complex space. The perihelion of Mercury was taken to be solely due to a relativity effect.

The Fitzgerald contraction was first observed empirically by astronomers, but Einstein derived it from an even simpler empirically observed relation: $x = Ct$, where x is any spatial distance and t is the time taken by a light signal to cover that distance, C being the velocity of light. The contraction is generally expressed as being equal to:

$$\sqrt{1 - \frac{v^2}{C^2}}$$

where v is the velocity of any object along the line of measurement. By applying Newtonian principles and algebraic manipulation, it

---

*A. Einstein, *Relativity* (London: Methuen and Co., Ltd., 1920) 115–26.

was possible to obtain an expression for the kinetic energy of a moving body, according to a simple series:

$$mC^2 + m\,(v^2/2) + (3/8)(m)(v^4/C^2) + \ldots,$$

where m is the mass and v is the velocity of the body. Obviously if the body were at rest only the first term would apply; so that the intrinsic energy of the body is mC^2. It should be obvious from simple mechanics that this energy, mC^2 is kinetic. How otherwise could the factor be a product of mass and velocity? Further it appears extremely likely that mC^2 is the sum of two equal kinetic energies $2[(\frac{1}{2}mC^2]$. Of course wave mechanics gives no sort of interpretation. Its waves are identified as probabilities; and its apologists are at pains to deny that its waves are in any sense "real." On the other hand, the theory of relativity exactly predicts a real wave relation. It is worth comparing this with another simple wave: that produced by a kink running along a taut string. The mass of the string wave is the product of its wavelength λ, say, and its mass per unit length k, say, where k is a constant, so that the forward kinetic energy of the wave is: $\frac{1}{2}k\lambda v^2$, where v is the constant velocity of the kink along the string. Of course the wave is not only moving forward at velocity v, but it is also vibrating transversely. So that the kinetic energy of vibration is momentarily also $\frac{1}{2}k\lambda v^2$. Thus the total energy of the wave is twice $\frac{1}{2}k\lambda v^2$, which comes to exactly mv^2 where λM is the mass of the wave. The kinetic energy of the string wave is only momentarily equal to Mv^2; but according to the first law of thermodynamics, energy is never lost; it only changes form. Half the kinetic energy of the string wave is in constant alternation into the less evident form of potential energy. When its vibration becomes static, the positive and negative charges located in its molecular fine structure are momentarily drawn slightly further apart; the work* done being equivalent to $\frac{1}{2}Mv^2$. We looked at the string wave because it supplied the simplest and clearest example—a wave swaying along a single dimension. But even multidimensional waves follow the same rule: all combine translation with rotation and all obey Hooke's law: stress is proportional to strain. In explaining the waves underlying $E = mC^2$, it is difficult to be sure how many

*For those not conversant with mechanics, work is force times distance. Force itself is mass times acceleration, while the latter is the dividend of the space covered by the square of the time: dimensions $M \times S^2 \div T^2$. These are exactly those of work.

dimensions might be involved; but the precise number is immaterial. According to Einstein a four-dimensional Euclidian space with $\sqrt{-1}$ (Ct) as the time coordinate x,y,z, $\sqrt{-1}$ (Ct) completely determinies our four-dimensional world existence. But if this were so, many positive quantities: mass, energy, including work, force, power, et cetera, should turn out negative, which is directly contrary to experience. Having spent thirty years with "field" theory, trying to reconcile relativity with wave mechanics, it seems extraordinary that he did not recognise $E = mC^2$ as the underlying wave relation, which also defines a particle. And it is also amazing that he did not see it as interpreting electromagnetism, especially after having recognised C as the final limiting straight velocity. Angular motion is in every way the counterpart of straight. All Newton's laws and equations have their exact, circular analogues, so that we should again expect a material atom to be both translating and gyrating at C.

Matter is simply made up of positive and negative electricity. There are many strong reasons for believing that all atoms are actually progressing at C. Relativity teaches that such velocities completely depend on the assigned frame of reference. But time has shown that there is only one specially significant frame: that with its origin at the centre of the whole cosmos. From this origin all atoms are flying away at the speed of light. This is the clear interpretation of the big bang theory.

The very adjective *astronomical* proclaims that cosmic distances have been steadily increasing over the last 2×10^{10} years. Thus Olber's paradox is resolved; the spiral arms and oblations of extragalactic nebulae explained; and the Fitzgerald contraction becomes a rider on Pythagoras. Even more satisfying is the fit with electromagnetism. How, then, does (1) also explain the coming into existence of the three primary particles—neutrons, protons, and electrons? First, we must accept a static, time- and temperature-free substratum, an underlying yet particulate field. We have to assume that that the ultimate, four-dimensional particles are also capable of some deformation. We might, for the sake of brevity, call them "micres" because of an underlying similarity with the micelles of biology; and also because "microhyperspheres" is such a mouthful.

118

The Generation of a Neutron

We imagine far into the past that a micre might have received energy in the form of spin. Energy implies inertia; and its influence generally flows from the centre outwards to the exterior. At the same time we should expect the acceleration of an equal and reverse spin on an adjacent micre. Spin seems to imply spiralling into the future. But there is no logical reason why there should not be a reverse, "widdershin" spiral pointing towards the past. And we should expect a sharp, physical difference between these two spins. Forward spin might generate an outward tension equivalent to a negative electric field; whereas the reverse spin could produce an opposite inward pressure balanced by the continued influx of energy. Thus we could visualise the opposites avoiding each other; but only by a slight margin. Paradoxically the two particles would be mutually attracted both electrically and magnetically, gradually approaching over untold eons. There is a fundamental difference between these opposites. Negative expansion would suffer outward restraint in accord with quantum theory, whereas positive growth could be held, layer by layer, by the deposition of inertial matter on the inner boundaries of shells. Finally, at some critical stage, the opposites may have fused into one concentric shell virtually forming a primal nonatomic-sized neutral particle: a neutron. Here we get an inkling as to why a proton is so much more massive than its opposite electron. Inside a proton there is room for inertia. Whereas the inside of an electron holds nothing but a hypervacuum, yet its exterior is held by an iron grip.

It is now possible to express these attractions quantitatively, and to equate them with measurable centrifugal force. Thus the nearest possible approach of two opposite micres may be d cm, where d is the diameter of a micre. The generated outward centrifugal force thus becomes $(2\ m\ C^2)/d$ dynes while its electrical attraction for its opposite positive is also known to be e^2/d^2 dynes. Equating these, we get:

$$d = e^2/(2\ mC^2)$$

where e is the charge on an electron, and m its mass in gm. This gives $d = 1.4 \times 10^{-13}$ cm, which is far too close to Rutherford's value for the diameter of an atomic nucleus not to be significant.

We can now visualise the background to existence as an ocean of neutrons. How did such a scene unfold to initiate the big bang and begin life, with all the complexity of a time sequence? We have to see neutrons as very slight dipoles. These concentric poles are spinning contrawise; so there must be a slender space between. Hence the dipolarity and, with it, slight gravitation.

In Chapter 5 the relation between electricity and gravity was quantitatively assessed and shown to be precisely equivalent to the curvature of space/time. Both Eddington and Dirac attempted to assess gravity against electricity and both obtained exceedingly large figures for the superiority of electric force over gravitation. Where they went astray was in starting with a neutral hydrogen atom instead of a neutral hydrogen molecule. Both a proton and an electron show inertia; but an electron alone is not subject to gravity. It is quite an unjustifiable assumption to take the inertial mass of an electron as being equivalent to its gravitational mass. The advantage of taking a neutral hydrogen molecule is that both the gravitational attraction of its two hydrogen atoms and their electric repulsions are exactly known. If this calculation is made, electricity is found to be 1.24×10^{36} times the force of gravity. The curvature of space/time was also shown to be $1.25 \times 10^{36} : 1$. Dipolar attraction is likewise proportional to the curvature of space/time, and thus it accurately and quantitatively accounts for gravitation.

Having shown that an ocean of neutrons would be subject to gravity, we must expect that given sufficient time, the particles would aggregate together until they formed the unstable equivalent of an outsized neutron star. The big bang then ensured an excessive ebulition of energy, releasing equal numbers of both electrons and protons, sending them along with residual neutrons far and wide into space. We have now seen how the three primary particles began to form the basis for all the ninety-two natural chemical elements. More importantly, there was also sufficient energy to impel and spin all the particles at the velocity of light, and to initiate time as a cardinal factor in existence.

Relativity, and its emphasis on $E = mC^2$ certainly revolutionised our concept of the physical world. Unfortunately, it also pervaded a very depressing and disheartening influence, because it claimed to debunk many individual and personal values. All frames were equivalent; any one observer was as good as another. Many cynical intellectuals began to chant: "There are no absolutes nor ultimates." If the rise of science in the seventeenth century deposed man from his high earthly centrepiece, Relativity seemed to rub his nose in the mire. On the contrary more careful consideration revealed $E = mC^2$ as a great liberator of the human spirit. Any man by a slight exertion of willpower, is able to lift a two-gallon bucket of water and move it at least a metre. Such a mass might be about 20 lbs or 10 kilos, which according to $E = mC^2$ is equivalent to 10^{25} ergs, or 10^{18} joules, or about a million billion horsepower. This little sum shows just how much more significant is the human spirit than inanimate matter, which has no power over itself. The calculation immediately poses the question: What is this willpower that is potentially so powerful? According to psychology, all human actions are emotive; but there is a presiding, central self-regarding emotion able to win any decision. Emotions are triggered by sense perception. But what sets off the master spirit? Here we should return to the behaviour of the hydrogen molecule and its system of two protons with two electrons.

These paired electrons are coordinated in that, together, they may complete an inert, helium structure about either proton, giving the most elementary example of hydrogen bonding. What could unite two simple but mutually averse negative charges and induce them to oscillate in pairs? We earlier harmonised relativity with electrons spinning at an ultimate C. But such an intense potential would certainly initiate sufficient magnetism to cause pairing; in fact it could easily evoke the formation of the covalent bonds so essential to organic chemistry.

Further, such bonds are not only basic to chemistry; they are the foundation of life itself. We hear a lot about the nucleotide helix, with its double spirals forming the ultimate genes responsible for heredity. The fine structures of such spirals are held together transversely by hydrogen bonds. We saw earlier that there is another helix, not so well publicised, which embraces the alpha proteins, the building blocks of life: the Pauling Helix. These helices link together all living structures; here the H-links are not transverse but longitudinal. They are rhythmically and centrally coordinated to form our human personalities; they act along the fibres and linear molecules of our own bodies. How is it then that these pulses have not been electrically detected? Here we must go back to the simple electron and its ultimate diameter of only 1.4×10^{-13} cm.

What is its frequency? We can find this very simply by dividing C by the above diameter times π; giving the extraordinary number 1.3×10^{-24}, a thousand times greater than that of the shortest gamma ray. This calculation gives a clue to the age-old body/mind problem. It uncovers a rationale that reconciles science and religion. gion.

The Simplicity of Wave Mechanics

We saw how relativity exemplified simple harmonic motion. And so, in a complex way, does the Shrödinger equation. Both give rise to distinct wave systems, clashing to give indeterminate results. We discerned a clear difference between waves from the big bang —those from $E = m\,C^2$ and atoms and secondary waves, E/M waves, those from radio light, and heat. These secondaries take part in all measurement; and make up our "Flatland," space/time existence. But they lack depth of being. Let us see the Earth as a liner in space. It faces the deep, elusive swell of the ocean; although it itself produces superficial waves and receives unpredictable reflections.

People hear about our subject: these "famous equations," and long to make sense of them. They already sweat under a costly "establishment" in the general grinding struggle to keep alive. All they get back is depression, fog, and condescension. It is a bit like the worries of a train traveller in the days of Bradshaw. Then all U.K. was covered by a web of lines. The traffic was dense enough to make a thick, dry-as-dust paper tome of tables: times and places for five or six competing lines. Some know-it-alls professed to be able quickly to grasp the respective merits of half a dozen different ways of getting from A to B; but the ordinary user was nonplussed and fogged. Yet all the while Bradshaw covered up an underlying world of romance and excitement on the "iron-road!" Soon every locality had its own ABC. timetable to save locals from the toils of Bradshaw. The present essay is offered as a general escape from the toils of mathematics.

Chapter 13

Thunderstorms, Auroras, and the Weather

Everyone talks about the weather,
but nobody does anything about it.
—Charles D. Warner

When electric discharges were first applied to the attenuated air of Geissler tubes, their peculiar light was said to appear as "flickering striae." It was not long before a close resemblance to auroras was clearly discerned. It was concluded that electrons arriving from space were attracted to the Earth's magnetic poles to produce large-scale displays of cathode light. Later both protons and electrons were observed radiating from the sun as the 'solar wind'; the former being predominant. Their connection with thunderstorms may invoke a basic principle of mechanics: the difference between mass and weight. And the reason may lie in the fundamental duality of electricity: positive and negative. If electrons are continuously striking upwards from Earth to cloud, how may their stock be replenished?

A further elementary principle is that there are only two ways in which a body can move: straight or turning about an axis. In recent years there has been a trend towards separating physics into two divisions—classical and modern. The first is based on Newton's laws and simple mechanics. The latter began with the French sceptics of the eighteenth century, leading to complex mathematics with Relativity as its apotheosis. Nevertheless the latter accounted very accurately for straight motion and the remarkable compressions and increases in inertia that arise when a body approaches the velocity of light, C. Relativity is based on the electrical structure of matter, and its success ought to spur us to ask if there might not also be some remarkable transformations when a particle increases its spin to the limit. We should begin by spinning the smallest and most elementary of particles. It was simple Newtonian mechanics that pointed the way to this ultimate minimum. Newton was one of the first great atomists. He established three cardinal laws of motion; but remarkably these apply equally to rotation as well as to direct transfer. Thus, with every active torque, there arises an equal and opposite reverse torque.

These six laws suggest that there must also be six basic degrees of freedom. And these six freedoms open the way to the Phase Rule and the Kinetic Theory of Gases; which in turn led to the exploration of what happened when the last traces of heat energy (molecular motion) drained away. It was directly observed that energy is particulate; that there are ultimate units or atoms of energy—quanta. All this kinetic development is built into the established nexus of science. Energy arises from the play of three dimensions: mass, space, and time. So its individuality leads to the idea of indivisible units of space: space-quanta. What might be the radius of such a quantum? When Rutherford first shot alpha particles through a thin sheet of aluminium, he was surprised to find that the "hard, massy" units of matter were mostly empty. He went on to estimate that the nucleus of an atom occupied only about a 10^5 part of the whole. A provisional figure for the nuclear radius is given as 1.4×10^{-13} cm. This is the least particle radius known; and we might also expect it to be that of a space quantum.

Since quanta are really "uncutable" they are a focus for thought about ultimate spin. According to relativity a space quantum translated at C might form a proton, giving a series of jumps like those of a digital clock: one space quantum per time quantum. Similarly a spinning quantum might lap at C in three dimensions, all its mass becoming concentrated in its surface. This ultimate spin would set up an immense centrifugal force equal to $m\,(C^2/r)$, where m is its enhanced mass, and r its radius. There should thus be an equal and opposite centripetal force acting towards the centre of spin; and this might well be the universal force of electricity. Just as the translating quantum becomes a photon; so the spinning quantum may become an electron. Fortunately we know exactly how many dynes it could exert in these circumstances : e^2/r^2, where e is the charge on the electron and r its radius of spin.

We can now make up an equation balancing centrifugal and centripetal forces. Thus :

(1), $mC^2/r = e^2/r^2$

Centrifugal force = Electric centripetal force

So that: (2), $m = e^2/C^2r$

Taking r to be : 1.4×10^{-13} cm,* we get by calculation : $m = 10^{-26}$ gm; by direct inertial observation : $m = 10^{-27}$ gm, a coincidence that is unlikely to be accidental. But it illuminates the close relation between electromagnetic light (photons) and individual electrons. We have seen that the mass of the former is about one 10^{-18} of that of the electron; so that photons of high frequency (10^{19}, X-rays) should provide enough energy (mass) to produce an electron—the Compton Effect.

We can now get an insight as to how the first atoms might have been created. We might start with an extensive ocean of empty space quanta, the backcloth of existence, limited only by space and time. To this came an infusion of energy: first quanta then electrons; to give the initial separation of positive and negative centres only 10^{-13} cm apart, the prototypyes of all atoms—neutrons. At the time of the Big Bang there may have been sufficient effused energy to further separate the opposed centres, giving off free protons and electrons. Force arises by an influx of acceleration causing a clockwise turning in space and time towards future being. The third law of motion is supreme; so that every acceleration generates an equal anticlockwise deceleration in the direction of past being.

*Encyclopedia of Science and Technology, McGraw Hill.

Thus the past is in process of storing a mirror-image record of future being: whatever happens in thought, word or deed in the future is stored in the past for ever.

Whatever the origin of free electrons and protons, we know that the solar wind is mainly composed of the two types. Both particles start off from the sun at the great speeds consistent with its very high temperature. But because protons are nearly 2,000 times more inertially massive, they are correspondingly slower than their co-generated electrons. The latter have been known to reach one fifth C; and because they may have no gravitational weight, they should not be retarded by the gravity of either sun or the other planets. Why, then, should they be so evident in auroras? Although weightless, they may nevertheless be deflected inertially by both magnetic and electric fields. Thus the initial stream of protons forming the solar wind might be able to attract a distant retinue of fast-moving electrons.

Protons have both mass and weight, so that they are gravitationally attracted to Earth along with their flying electrons. The process could resemble the fractional separation of alcohol from water. The latter is strongly associated, so that its aggregates move more slowly than the lighter and faster alcohol molecules. Separation by distillation then becomes possible. Protons and electrons are gradually separated before they reach Earth. The former come in towards the equator, while the faster electrons are deflected by the Earth's magnetic poles. Here their presence in the stratosphere induces auroras.

The fate of incoming protons is more complex. At the equator they will be met by rising streams of dissociated water molecules. Each proton may attach itself to a simple water molecule through a lone pair of electrons from the oxygen atom. At some point condensation will commence to form the base of a cloud. Other faster-moving, dissociated molecules will rise above the cloud base to meet incoming protons and become positively charged. The cloud will become typically cumulus. In its higher reaches there will be two opposed forces: association induced by lower temperature and dispersion actuated by positive charges. Eventually condensation will occur to form charged water droplets. These will finally sink within the cloud and join its base, which will become increasingly positively charged. The process will continue until electrons from the ground will strike upwards causing a lightning flash, reducing the charge on the base and triggering a downpour.

An Electric Cycle in Nature

A continued neutralisation would seem to move the Earth's potential away from neutrality. How might the drain of electrons be balanced? Incoming protons are each positively charged so that the narrowness of their equatorial band may become rapidly diffuse and broadened by mutual repulsion. After passing the cool air above the stratosphere, they could meet ascending single molecules of water vapour rising from the warm equator, so that one lone pair of electrons on each water-molecule could attract one positively charged proton. Such complexes could then drift, still at high altitude, away from the equator towards more temperate zones. At some point their positive charges would be strongly attracted by negatively charged water droplets arriving with ground-level air from the magnetic poles. Electrons from space might first ionise polar oxygen or nitrogen, before reducing some to charged atoms to give auroral effects; residual atoms recombining to form ozone and similar products. Anticyclonic air at the poles is generally very cold and dry. Electrons are likely to be carried with it to the earth's surface. Others may be co-opted by moisture droplets formed from the more humid and temperate air at lower latitudes. Obviously there should be a point where negative air at ground level blends with, and neutralises, descending positive complexes to give off atoms of active neutral hydrogen. The latter would then be free to unite with active oxygen donors such as ozone, forming water. This would then join the water released by its loss of charge. It is clear that descending polar electrons could make up the loss of those striking up towards thunderclouds so that there should be a continuous electric transference from poles to equator forming a well-dispersed, low-potential flow.

More specifically the North Atlantic shows an area of anticyclonic pressure, the North Atlantic Eddy, with its centre near the Azores. Warm air rises in the Gulf of Mexico and later streams eastwards parallel with the East Coast of America carrying positive charges. Finally it meets cold negative air originating near Baffin Bay, not far from the North Magnetic Pole. It is noteworthy that the sea between Cape Farewell and Labrador forms an area of almost permanent low pressure that breeds depressions. If the electric aspect of the weather is taken into account, it could provide an additional factor in the prediction of weather. The meeting and blending of positive and negative humidity might not necessarily give rise to spasmodic electric discharges. A more gradual neutralisation could take place with the deposition of rain, arising both by the combination of neutral hydrogen atom with activised oxygen, as well as the natural association of water molecules after loss of charge.

Chapter 14

Marie Corelli and World Peace

There was peace among the nations.
—Longfellow

The period before the First World War marked a great age for writers and novelists. Radio and television had not then been invented, but the printing press had been brought to an acme of perfection. Books could be produced and bought very cheaply. Most of the writers of that time confined themselves to simply telling fictional stories, novels; but there were a few who aspired to convert and educate the world to their point of view, e.g., H. G. Wells, G. B. Shaw, and Anatole France. A famous writer with a foot in both camps was Sir Arthur Conan Doyle with his *Sherlock Holmes* stories and spiritualism. Marie Corelli was also a celebrity and prophet of those days. Her home at Stratford on the road to Warwick became a famous shrine and was featured on the popular picture postcards.

What then was the particular message which she sought to put across? Her first book was titled *The Romance of Two Worlds*. It was first published in 1885, the same year as the discovery of X-rays by Röntgen. Those were great days in the development of electricity, and Marie Corelli seized on the new discoveries to put forward a novel way of reconciling life and thought. In fact the *Two Worlds* comprised, on the one hand the hard, material, everyday world we can all feel and touch; on the other was the "unseen" personal world of mind and spirit. She tried to demonstrate that the really important world was the "unseen," and her novels were based on this thesis. To be properly conscious of the "unseen" world of light and electricity was to be born anew. Thus in her last novel, *The Young Dianna*, which appeared in *Nash's* and *Pall Mall* magazines during the First World War, Dianna begins as an aging spinster who has been betrayed: "Poor old thing she must be *forty* if she's a day." Then she gets in with a professor who is able to distill energy from sunlight. She becomes young again and is able to find retribution by breaking the hearts of all the men she meets.

It is interesting to reflect on how her ideas were received. It is recorded in the Bible how the common people heard Jesus gladly; but the Pharisees plotted to destroy him. Similarly many ordinary people took the Corelli ideas as a boost for a kind of practical everyday Christianity. But the professors of physics and theology were much more scathing: "She had allowed her imagination to run away with her," they exlaimed. Even Gilbert and Sullivan, who were in process of presenting their famous light operas, gave her a sharp, stiletto jab in the *Mikado*: "I've got a little list of society offenders who might well be underground; . . . they never would be missed . . ." Then they go on, "the lady novelist . . . and she never, never would be missed."

At the time, not long after the pseudonyms adopted as "George Elliot" and "George Sands," Marie Corelli was the outstanding lady writer; and since that time women have increasingly come into their own by writing novels. The lines in question now seem hopelessly and outrageously dated.

What was so exciting about the Corelli philosophy was that it forms an excellent basis for a one-world ideology. All the faiths and creeds in the world hark back to some particular, founder-seer from the past. What saps their strength, and prevents them all from coming together and living in harmony, are the conflicting arguments that often arise from the records of history. Because electricity was a new force that everyone could easily appreciate and check by experiment, the warring discords could be all swallowed up. You may remember that when the United Nations was formed, one of its special agencies was set aside for education, science and culture: UNESCO. At the time, Aldous Huxley said that one of the great things lacking from the UN was a common ideology. We hear a lot in Coventry about one world, the one great cause; but you can't have one world without one all-embracing ideology. Much of the weakness of the UN follows from this great lack. All causes that have lasted and fired the imagination have always been based on an essential set of fundamental principles. We also hear a lot about reconciliation, but little about the yawning gap between science and the moral law. As a boy the writer soon realised that there were two main sources of truth about existence. But he also saw that they were, at best, in water-tight compartments, at worst, on collision course. Marie Corelli's *Two Worlds* offers an escape from this collision, a synthesis arising from opposed thesis and antithesis.

Inevitably the *Two Worlds* had a rough ride. Critics emphasised the romance: they thought her science was quite fanciful. As experimentation with electrical discharges went ahead, it became clear that electricity was not quite so mysterious as it first appeared. It was, in fact, composed of minute identical units, rather like atoms—electrons. Best of all, these particles could be deflected by both magnetic and electric centres. They seemed to be just like material atoms; and their materiality could be accurately measured by deflection. If a ship is deflected by a storm, its drift measures the size of the storm. Electrons turned out to be very small: only one-two-thousandth part of the smallest atom. Of course, no one could weigh them on a balance. But since Newton the inertia of a body has always been found to be proportional to its weight; and the inertia of electrons was determined very accurately. Electrons were simply sub-atomic particles:

> Fleas have fleas which on them prey,
> And these have lesser fleas to bite 'em,
> And so proceed ad infinitum.

The natural development and widespread use of electric power only increased the apparent materiality of the electron. Thus it was that the "Two Worlds" were forgotten. Electrons were material particles and formed an important component of the one hard, physical and material world. In fact everyone had jumped to the conclusion that because electrons were inert they were necessarily massive. Whereas you can, in fact, have inertia without mass, e.g., the gyroscope, the spinning top; which defy gravity by returning to their vertical axis when disturbed.

Sir Oliver Lodge was mostly on the side of Corelli. He believed in the luminiferous ether pervading all space; which fits in well with spiritualism and the "Two Worlds." More specifically he believed that the electron was an insubstantial hole in the ether maintained as a minute eddy. Because the nucleus of an atom is nearly two thousand times more massive than an electron, these latter may be crudely likened to the small amount of mortar binding a massive wall of bricks. The advent of the twentieth century saw the tide of science turn away from the ether. Atoms were no longer thought of as hard and durable. They were shown to be mostly empty, with minute positive and negative centres. The wall of bricks became a much more attenuated network; but electrons still held the mesh together. They also held the world together. More importantly, their pulsation held all living things together. In a dead, inorganic object, a stone for example, the electrons have already transferred to a set position. In contrast, when they take part in a rhythmical concerted vibration, their structure, animal or vegetable, becomes alive—this is the dance of life. Fibrous proteins and fibrous cellulose form the respective frameworks of animals . . . and plants. Their resonance bonds link with the nucleotides DNA and RNA.

There are three cogent reasons why electrons are nonmaterial:

1. Very large numbers are expelled from the sun every second (the solar wind). Were they material particles they ought to be gravitationally attracted by the giant planet Jupiter. This has not been observed.
2. According to relativity the energy of an atom is made up from two parts: nuclear and kinetic. Electronic energy belongs to the latter category.
3. The Universe is expanding, and its curvature is proportional to the gravitational constant, which generates only one 1.26×10^{-36} part of the equivalent electrical attraction. Exactly the same figure arises by comparing the radius of an atom with that of the universe.

Soon it was realised that the transfer of force across space was bound to take time, so that, if one atom approached another, it would move fractionally closer before the second atom began to feel the influence. This means that fast-moving objects must shrink along their lines of motion. Space and time, rather than space alone, must form the background to existence. It is right to describe time as running at right-angles to space. Otherwise a group of inanimate objects, Stonehenge for example, would change their relative positions with the lapse of time. But it is not good enough to describe an event by space and time alone. We do this when we enter a date in our diaries; and we know how uncertain such an entry may be. A real event has not only to have a place and a time; it also has to *be*, to be created. To just place space across time is like making a signpost without a prop, or a weathercock without a spire. Similarly the advice to forget ourselves, to cross out the I is not enough. We have to build on that cross; to express and assert the I. Only in this way may we make a unique contribution to the unity of existence.

The three cardinal axes of space, time, and being are endorsed by elementary mechanics. Velocity is change of position with time, giving a simple slope between two axes. Acceleration is a change of that slope; which means turning about a third axis at right angles to both space and time. These three contexts—*space, time,* and *being* form the basis for a more perfect and profound sphere, a hypersphere. We all live on its surface, which is expanding and forms a fleeting boundary between "seen" and "unseen" worlds. Electricity orders all events; and because it is the one supreme force originating all other forces, it unifies science by explaining heat, light, sound, magnetism, gravitation, the properties of matter and also clarifies the mechanisms of thought and action. It is the one factor that gives us hope for the future and rescues us from the desperation of an inexorable second law of thermodynamics. Either we see only decay and dissolution ahead, as expressed by Macbeth's famous lament, or we choose its counterpart with the parody:

Tomorrow, and tomorrow, and tomorrow,
Brings in its lesser triumphs day by day,
Recording them for all eternity;
And all our yesterdays have shown the wise
The challenge of an expanded life.

On, on, far-searching beacon,
Life's a daring venture, that crowds its appointed niche
Into the great canvass;
It is a saga planned by its author,
Full of concord, completing everything.

Epilogue

Can these dry bones live?
—Ezekiel, Chapter 37

Our Flattenened Lives: Thoughts on European Reconciliation

One of the most thought-provoking statements made at a recent conference* was that reconciliation implies release from mental shackles. To achieve reconciliation between East and West we have to find a single satisfying idea which will embrace two apparently opposed systems of thought. Further, any proposed solution also has to include and satisfy truths about the physical world (science).

The basic idea underlying Marxism is the view that the means of production (economics) condition the whole supra- and infra-structures of society. This seems to be a fragment of a much broader generalisation, because the means of production themselves are governed by scientific principles. And these in turn go much further into the past than is generally conceded. Thus the problem of motion, of how one object can change its position relative to another, has engaged men's attention right through from prehistory. Science itself began with reconciliation—release from slavery. Watching the stars enabled astronomers in Ancient Egypt to predict the Nile flood. This allowed the cultivation of increased areas, giving more food for less work—which paradoxically engendered slavery because it became profitable to enslave captives rather than to destroy them.

The slaves themselves began to think about release. And it

*Conference on European Reconciliation, Coventry Cathedral.

became clear that they would have to adopt rather strict personal rules, the Law of Moses, if they were to achieve it. Here again we see that it is verifiable truth which alters society, not just the immediate, inanimate tools of production. After the slaves had achieved their promised land, it soon became evident that the Law of Moses was not enough. Their leaders saw that their law must also take in the new knowledge (science) which continually arrived from the North (Greece). They began to realise the insidious danger of one person becoming enslaved to another through debt. There had to be a day of periodical release (reconciliation), a jubilee. Britain today is badly in need of a jubilee. Its national debt started when previous Stuart debts were extinguished by a consolidated fund (two and a half percent consols). This debt has never been paid off; on the contrary, it has increased to approximately a hundred billion pounds; also, many more debts have come into play. Shares are debts. Municipalities are in debt. Tenants are in debt. Civilisation is now almost completely polarised by debt.

It is clear that there is a coherent body of objective truth which is not static but which grows and evolves with the elapse of time. It is this truth which modifies and changes the whole structure of society. And it is this truth which brings reconciliation by showing how everyone should aspire to be free. This evolving and coherent body of truth forms a succession throughout history. It originated in Egypt; it grew into the Mosaic Law; it was further embellished by the Jewish prophets; and reached a climax with Jesus Christ. The Romans saw that conversion to Christianity was a clever device for governing their empire—their slaves might become much more docile and easy to direct. But after the collapse of Rome, the rise of Christendom enabled civilisation to move out of slavery.

The essence of life is light and being. It is not accidental that both Old and New Testaments start by stressing the importance of light. Yet the established churches have done little to discover what light is; in fact, they have sometimes suppressed optical research. Thus over the years they have lost their claim to account for the living pulse of the universe, becoming ossified and halfway towards complete fossilisation. It remained for Newton to suggest a corpuscular structure for light—and for Huygens to demonstrate its likeness to wave-motion. Newton established dynamics—which later blossomed into thermodynamics—and this explained heat in terms of the motion of ultimate particles, atoms and molecules. It is through thermodynamics that steam engines evolved; and these in turn helped to bring about the Industrial Revolution.

Thus we see how after a lapse of more than a thousand years, the evolution of truth reasserted itself. Newton is in the direct line of succession to Jesus Christ. He was a convinced but secret Unitarian; and he arranged that his conversion to that view should only be revealed two hundred years after his death because of the upset it might otherwise have caused. We may think that Newton was not true to himself by hiding his unitarianism, but it was regarded as a great heresy at the time and he could not have established his scientific laws without keeping his private belief secret. He considered that Jesus Christ radiated God rather than "was God," the monumental work being liberation from slavery: "I will show you the truth; and the truth shall make you free."

Who then was the successor prophet to Newton? A hundred years after Newton, the mantle fell on Alfred Russel-Wallace, the original discoverer of natural sellection. His paper had already been accepted when Darwin wrote to him to say that he had been thinking on similar lines—and they finally published a joint paper. Both Darwin and Russel-Wallace were expert naturalists and anthropologists, and both made long voyages round the world, Darwin to the Galapagos and Wallace to the Phillipines. Darwin became famous with his *Origin of Species;* but Wallace's *Man's Place in the Universe* has been forgotten. Darwin believed natural selection was a purely mechanical process, whereas Wallace adduced many reasons for thinking that the chances against the randomly inspired evolution of living organisms were so enormous as to be infinite.

To reinforce his ideas, Wallace quoted from Shakespeare, 150 years ago, the now almost trite excerpt:

What a piece of work is a man! How noble in reason! How infinite in faculty! . . . In action how like an angel! In apprehension how like a god!

139

Darwin saw nature as an impersonal machine, in keeping with the then burgeoning Industrial Revolution and with the prevailing establishment. Many of Wallace's statements would have now to be modified. For example, in those days Lord Kelvin thought from conventional cooling that the sun had been in existence only 15 million years, whereas today the figure is nearer 15,000 million. Also, Wallace thought our own galaxy was the universe, whereas it is but a grain, a unit. But he was prophetic in saying that most stars are either double or belong to a system such as the Pleiades—and also that the earth could be the only planet in the solar system capable of supporting life. The book remains a marvellous inspiration to scientists. His great point was that the sun was a quite exceptional star; that the Solar System had a very mysterious origin unsolved even to this day; that evolution involved a multiplying series of highly improbable chances.

What has religion and indeed all philosophy got to do with the mechanics of light? Most people think that the light mentioned in the Bible refers to the light of the mind, whereas it may be altogether more fundamental. For example, we ourselves, our souls and bodies, are waves, just as the units of light are waves. What is so special about light viewed as a type of wave-motion? Most waves are naturally longitudinal—waves on the sea, waves along a skipping-rope, the shunt-wave along a line of railway trucks, the sound of music. Light waves are special because they have lost their longitudinality.

The most unheralded but far-reaching finding of our time is the Fitzgerald contraction, whereby fast-moving objects contract in the direction of their motion. It is not generally realised that the diameter of the earth pulsates appreciably every six hours owing to its eighteen mile per second orbit round the sun. This discovery leads on to relativity, which in turn conditions all our lives because it says that any frame of reference is as good as any other. We are all predisposed to think our own frame is the most important. Thus self-centeredness by both individuals and nations is vastly engendered, and is responsible for many troubles.

What has the Lorentz contraction got to do with the nature of light? The waves of light are moving so fast that their extension lengthwise entirely disappears. They become concentrated into instantaneous pulses of a definite mass. This allows the measurement of the energy of a pulse; and it turns out that half this energy is due to forward motion and half due to spin. Because the units of light are material particles they have much in common with atoms; and all recent research demonstrates that just as the waves of light are particles, so the ultimate particles of matter (atoms) are waves. Just as the waves of light have lost their longitudinality, so the waves of matter have lost theirs—becuase, as with light, the energy conserved by atoms turns out to be: mC^2 (m, the mass of the atom, and C, the velocity of light). We saw that the waves of light were flattened into pulses; and so, we are led to think that our three-dimensional lives are also but flattened cross-sections of our real four-dimensional existence. We must believe that the universe is basically four-dimensional—and that the passage of time is but a temporary flattening. Wave-flattening implies resurgence and recovery into an expanded, more abundant life. Eventually our bodies will complete their wave-cycle; they will decompose into their elements leaving bones or ash. The question is: "Can these remnants, these dry bones, live?" From what science has already discovered about the physical world there is a great probability that they can and will.